Say Their

[signature]

*Spoke @ HQ
Best Buy HQ
11.13.2024
for Think Blue event
Part of Native American History Month*

FOREWORD

My name is Ramona Marozas, and I'm a proud Bad River Band of Lake Superior Chippewa Indians tribal member. I am touched that a non-Native person of the dominant population is illuminating an epidemic of Indian Country that is plaguing our communities. I think it would be difficult to find a member of a tribal community that doesn't know someone impacted by the crippling epidemic Bonnie Bley writes about: Missing and Murdered Indigenous Persons (MMIP), Missing and Murdered Native Americans (MMNA), Murdered Indigenous Women (MMIW), etc...

Bley's manuscript focuses on the experiences within this epidemic; it's raising awareness of Selena Bell Not Afraid's story and others. This manuscript raises awareness and illuminates first-hand perspectives from family members and friends of a Crow and Northern Cheyenne tribal members who were killed, as well as those who are working to make a difference in Indian Country with the goal of lessening instances of violence against Native women and men.

Bley's work is illuminating a specific population of Indian Country - women - in this all too large epidemic impacting probably all Native peoples across Indian Country in some way. Many studies certainly pinpoint and are focused specifically on Native females and have been released by Native-focused organizations gathering data surrounding women and girls.

For example, this one was released by the Urban Indian Health Institute:

STOLEN

VOICES

<u>MISSING AND MURDERED</u>

<u>IN BIG HORN COUNTY</u>

By Bonnie Bley

https://www.uihi.org/wp-content/uploads/2018/11/Missing-and-Murdered-Indigenous-Women-and-Girls-Report.pdf

And Minnesota's groundbreaking MMIW task force report:

https://dps.mn.gov/divisions/ojp/Documents/missing-murdered-indigenous-women-task-force-report.pdf

"Indigenous women, girls, and two-spirit people are far more likely to experience violence, be murdered, or go missing compared to other demographic groups in Minnesota. While Indigenous people make up just 1% of the state's population, 9% of all murdered girls and women in Minnesota from 2010-2019 were American Indian."

This does not mean Native men and other Native people of different ages/genders are discluded from cases of missing people and violence, of course. Here are some very important excerpts from an Operation Lady Justice Report to the President in 2020:

https://operationladyjustice.usdoj.gov/sites/g/files/xyckuh281/files/media/document/operation-lady-justice-report-508_final.pdf

"The report describes a productive first year of task force operations, during which we heard from Tribal leaders, public safety officials, community advocates, and concerned citizens about the extraordinary public safety challenges facing Native Americans across the country — in particular, the disappearance of Tribal members and the incidence of fatal violence suffered by Native men, women, and children."

"... the Task Force on Missing and Murdered American Indians and Alaska Natives, also known as Operation Lady

Justice (OLJ). The Task Force, which includes seven members from the U.S. Departments of Justice (DOJ), Interior, and Health and Human Services, is focused on improving the criminal justice process with respect to missing and murdered American Indian and Alaska Natives, especially missing and murdered women and girls."

"Violence has become a far-too-prevalent feature of life in American Indian and Alaska Native communities, but we remain determined to work with American Indian and Alaska Native nations to make sure it is not permanent. Through the work of Operation Lady Justice and thanks to your leadership, Native Americans are forgotten no more. Thank you for the opportunity to share in your Administration's pursuit of justice for all Native Americans."

Bonnie Bley's manuscript is just one of the many writings that ensure Selena Bell Not Afraid's and others' stories will not be forgotten.

Ramona Marozas

Bad River Band of Lake Superior Chippewa Indians

Renowned Native American Journalist

About the Author

Bonnie Bley, a native of Wyoming, spent her formative years in the border reservation town of Hardin, MT, situated in the southeastern corner of Montana. Her educational journey took her to Aberdeen, SD, and Bloomington, MN, where she honed her skills and knowledge. In the late 1980s, she made Minnesota her home, and to this day, it remains the backdrop to her life.

Although Minnesota has become her primary residence, Bonnie remains deeply connected to her roots in Montana and Wyoming, considering them the bedrock of her identity. It is within this intricate tapestry of her experiences that Bonnie Bley has woven the compelling narrative of "Stolen Voices: Missing and Murdered in Big Horn County." This poignant work sheds light on the stories of Indigenous People who have tragically gone missing or been murdered in the very county where she spent her upbringing, offering a heartfelt exploration of a community's struggles and losses.

Acknowledgment

I would like to extend my heartfelt gratitude and appreciation to Shane Small, Paula Castro, Nate Stops, Cheryl Horn, Cary Lance, Audra, Trista Fog In The Morning, Jennifer White Bear, Jennifer Pipe, Ramona Marozas, Sovereign Bodies Institute, Kathy Lekse, Larry Colton, Lt. Colonel Dave Grossman, Gary Liming, Nicole O'Shea, Mona Pond, Maxine Sangrey, Jolene Rides Horse, Tronnes Birdin Ground, Rebecca Sweeney, and Kaylene Red Wolf for without you this project would not have been possible.

I would also like to extend a special Thank You to my immediate family and close friends for your never-ending support and love.

Thank you to my team at NY Publishers for all the hard work and dedication to this project.

This book is dedicated to all the women, girls, men, boys, and two-spirit Indigenous people who have gone missing or been murdered. Your stories will not be forgotten.

Contents

A Crow Prayer

(Free Translation by Robert H. Lowie - June 12, 1883 – September 21, 1957 - Austrian-born American anthropologist who was an expert on North American Indians. He was instrumental in the development of modern anthropology and has been described as "one of the key figures in the history of anthropology.")

I used to think that since my birth, I had many sorrows. It turns out that there was something in store for me. I was grieving, but I did not know that today, all manner of sorrow would be coming to a head. The women at my home are miserable, I daresay. "How are the Crow faring?" they are continually thinking to themselves. My poor dear housemates, my distressed kin, the enemy makes them sit under the dripping water; he is ever abusing them. He thinks his men are the only ones to be brave. What can I do to distress him, I wonder?

You Above, if there be one who knows what is going on, repay me today for the distress I have suffered. Inside the Earth, if there be anyone who knows what is going on, repay me for the distress I have suffered. The One Who causes things, whoever He be, I have now had my fill of life. Grant me death; my sorrows are over-abundant. Though children are timid, they die harsh deaths, it is said. Though women are timid, you make them die harsh deaths. I do not want to live long; were I live long, my sorrows would be over-abundant. I do not want it.

1

Stolen Voices

It was three o'clock in the morning on a Friday night. I was desperately trying to sleep. I had been deeply troubled the entire week by the shocking news that the body of sixteen-year-old Selena Bell Not Afraid had been discovered twenty days after she had been reported missing on New Year's Day.

It wasn't simply that I was just troubled by this tragic news, but it was Selena who was keeping me awake. I didn't know Selena. I've never met her, but yet here she was delivering a message for me to hear. She was pretty persistent.

She whispered to me, "Get up and tell my story. My story and the stories of my sisters and brothers need to be told to everyone. We need you to help be our voices that have been stolen."

At first, I tried to ignore her. I drifted in and out of sleep. She kept nagging at me, not letting go. I finally succumbed to her pleas after an hour and a half of tossing and turning. I wondered why and how I could possibly help. I threw back the covers and sat up. I rubbed the sleep out of my half-opened eyes. I got out of bed and staggered towards my living room. I fired up my laptop and started researching.

My research proved to be unending, unrelenting, jaw-dropping, gut-wrenching, unbelievable, yet rewarding at the same time. Like any research project, I started with what was in front of me and what I knew. Then, I followed the trail of bread crumbs in every direction possible. I felt as though the bread crumb trail was never-ending.

I reached out to old friends and strangers, who ended up becoming friends because, in the end, we all want the same thing. An end. An end to the madness in the world around us, especially when it hits so close to home. The increasing frequency becomes more apparent as it's happening right in front of us. It's happening to people we know and love. Pushing the news away becomes more and more difficult, as it's starting to affect us directly. When something affects us directly, we are more inclined to sit up and pay attention. When something affects us directly, it becomes harder to deflect the impact it has on our hearts.

I followed social media intently. I looked at the photos of young girls, women, and men who have gone missing and those who have been murdered. I looked into their eyes and saw the same thing I saw in photos of myself at their age. I saw the look of happiness. I saw the look of bright futures and dreams of things bigger than themselves. I was able to connect faces to names.

Daily, I scoured news feeds and social media chatter. I followed it from day one. I had no idea that New Year's Day 2020 would be the day that would change so many of our lives. The few people who I had confided in about my project were sending me updates. Some days, it was almost hourly, making sure I didn't miss a thing. One evening, I watched a bone-chilling video one of my friends had shared. The video was a gaunt, unkempt Caucasian homeless man speaking into the camera of his phone in a small enclosed room with only a wall and what appeared to be a closet door in view.

He was delivering a message that sent chills up and down my spine. It was incredibly disturbing. As I listened, I tried to process the information he was putting out there. It felt like hearing Ted Bundy talk about his crimes for the first time.

This man was talking about women who had gone missing and never been found. He claimed to know where hundreds of human remains of missing persons were. He talked about a road between twenty and thirty miles outside of town where he claimed so many human remains were located. I intently tried to map this location out in my brain. I couldn't exactly pin it down. He kept referring to it as the farming road just to the west.

The video didn't last more than five minutes. I decided I would watch this again later and try to process what I had just seen and heard. I put my phone down and stood up. I slowly ran my fingers through my hair and said out loud, "What the hell did I just hear?"

A few hours later, I went back to my friend's Facebook page, who shared the video. The message "this content has been removed" flashed on his page in place of the video. I reached out to a couple of people who I noticed had commented on the post. They were just as shocked as I was. I was able to find out through one of my connections his name and information. I was informed that he was arrested in 2017 in connection with a murdered Native American Indian woman in Colorado. This led to so many questions.

I located a private Facebook page group that was created in June 2020 and has only two members. A young woman and a man. The young woman is the moderator. The home page includes a photo of the man next to a mirror that reads in childlike print, "Homeless and Human."

I was able to find his Facebook page and his YouTube channel through this moderator. He's made hundreds of videos that take countless hours to view. He continues to make videos in which he references the names of the missing and murdered – including the young woman whose murder he was implicated, yet exonerated as someone else came forward and confessed to her murder.

It was hard to avoid being distracted by his ramblings because of his ghastly appearance and the disorganized and chaotic display in the background in his videos. The more I watched and listened, I wondered if he truly was a misunderstood, mentally ill homeless man trying to help and provide answers. Or does he know more than he's leading on? The more I listened, the more I was haunted by his words and his face.

I tuned him out and forced his words and image to the back of my head. I didn't reach out to him or the woman who seemed to be the only friend he had in this virtual world. I'm unsure how credible or mentally stable he is. He'd most likely lead me down a dangerous rabbit hole I won't be able to escape. I turned my focus and energy elsewhere.

Some of the people I reached out to didn't want to talk. The subject matter was too difficult. They wanted to put this all behind them. While those rejections were rather disappointing and felt like a dagger through the middle of my project, I found the majority of people I reached out to were more than willing to talk. Some of my friends connected me with incredible people that I now call friends. I listened to them tell their stories. "I'm in" was the response they gave when I reached out. They agreed it is time for these stories to be heard.

January 20th, 2020, was a day just like any other Monday. I hit snooze on my alarm clock three times before getting out of bed and going through my daily morning routine. I trudged to work, completely unaware of how much this day would shake my core. This was the day sixteen-year-old Selena was found dead from what officials initially deemed was caused by hypothermia.

I had been following the story of her disappearance since January 1st via my Facebook page. She was from the same small town in which I had grown up in. She also attended the same High School I did so many years ago. Her relatives are former classmates of mine, which is why she kept appearing on my Facebook feed. My friends shared her story and updates on the search on a daily basis so that she was not forgotten - and just vanish into the wind like so many before her. It was impossible for me to ignore her story. Not only was her presence on this earth a daily pop-up on my social media feed, but she was not the first one to go missing and be found dead later in my hometown community.

Several other teenage girls had their lives taken much too soon before the day Selena mysteriously vanished. They popped up on my social media feeds as well. I remember seeing them, and feeling sorry for the families of those girls, and feeling blessed that this was not my life. I offered up my thoughts and prayers to my friends for the families in their comments section. Then, I moved on with my day. Being that I no longer live in the area, I was unable to offer up any help besides offerings of thoughts and prayers.

The reason Selena was the one to finally grab my attention to this epidemic is because her loved ones kept her name out in the forefront of social media. Honestly, if it wasn't popping up on my social media feed from the people in my hometown, I too would be oblivious to this horrendous problem facing Native

American Indians in the United States and First Nations People in Canada.

Their stories sometimes make the local papers, but the issue with that is that only the local people in those areas are aware of what's going on. It hasn't been until recently that their stories have begun to reach a national audience. Before Selena Not Afraid, the missing and murdered Native American Indian girls and women have been buried between the headlines of local papers.

In order to get a real grasp of the hidden epidemic which has been taking place for decades, even centuries, to women on Indian Reservations and beyond, you have to take a look at the staggering and shocking statistics put out by the CDC, the US Justice Department, Montana Department of Justice, the Association of American Indian Affairs, the National Congress of American Indians Report, and Sovereign Bodies Institute. While it is tragically true that men, women, and children go missing or are murdered on a daily basis, Native American Indian women are murdered on reservations and nearby areas at more than ten times the national average for all races. [5] Homicide is now the third leading cause of death for Native American Indian girls and young women aged 10-34. It is the sixth leading cause of death for those between the ages of 20-44. 75% of these homicides were committed by family members, friends, or acquaintances.

Eighty-four percent of American Indian and Alaska Native women have experienced violence in their lifetime. [3] An astounding one out of every six American women have been the victim of rape or attempted rape in her lifetime. [1] This statistic is one that hits close to home for me. Twice in my life, I was the victim of attempted rape. The first time, I was fifteen, and the second time, I was eighteen. On both occasions, I knew the man who tried to rape me.

I never talked it about to anyone with the exception of maybe one close friend. A girl always needs a shoulder to cry on. I pushed the incidents behind me and forged on as if nothing had happened, as I had narrowly escaped from the horror of being raped on both occasions. Even though, between the two instances, it included my face, neck, and chest having whisker burns from the man's beard of my first perpetrator and rug-burned elbows and a pair of torn panties from my second perpetrator.

The only thing both instances had in common was they left me with a sense of shame and guilt. Although, I felt as if I was one of the lucky ones as I had evaded being totally and completely violated. If I could just push the memory of it down and lock it away, I could move on from it. I looked on the brighter side of things and knew that somewhere out there was someone much worse off than me. I've always found my silver linings, even in the worst of situations. It's a basic human survival tactic.

The rate of rape for Native American Indian women is one out of every three, which equates to 34.1% compared to their other racial counterparts. 18.8% of African-American women, 17.7% of Caucasian, and 14.6% of Hispanic women are victims of rape in their lifetime. [1]

The sad fact of these numbers is that so many rapes go unreported for fear of retaliation, public shame, and humiliation. The percentage of victims is most likely higher than reported. Rape is more likely to go unreported when the offender is a boyfriend, friend, or acquaintance.

Only 6% of rapists serve any time in jail for their crimes, which is also why so many women who survive rape do not come forward and press charges. [2] They would rather just wash it away in the shower and put it all behind them. They put on a brave face, hide the internal pain and sometimes external injuries, and move on. Rape victims are three times more likely to suffer from depression, four times more likely to contemplate suicide, thirteen times more likely to abuse alcohol, and twenty-six times more likely to abuse drugs. [2]

We need to be attentively conscious of the vital need to address grief and trauma that is occurring with Native American Indian girls and women. We need to be cognizant that psychological healing cannot take place without protecting their physical safety.

Until recently, there wasn't any particular terminology to describe the sudden disappearances and violent deaths of the Native American Indian people, whether they be daughters, mothers, sisters, sons, or fathers intertwined into everyday life. Behind the vanishing women is a myriad of causes ranging from domestic violence, sex trafficking, police indifference, racism, alcohol and drug use to lack of resources set aside by tribal governments and complex jurisdictional issues between tribal, federal, and local law enforcement agencies.

The Sovereign Bodies institute is trying to change all that. Annita Lucchesi, a Southern Cheyenne cartographer and human trafficking survivor, has been diligently working on building a comprehensive database to better track the missing and murdered. She's waded through red tape to get the data. She has had to rely on news reports, law enforcement data, government missing person databases, and information shared by families and members of the community.

The data has been insufficient up to this date because keeping such information has not been centralized. She has discovered through her research that this problem has persisted for generations. Most cases remain unsolved. Many were never reported. Many were never investigated or investigations fell short of giving the families any solid answers. In some of the cases, the victims were misclassified as white or another race.

New Mexico, Washington, Arizona, Alaska, and Montana have the highest number of cases of missing or murdered on record. [7] In Montana, Native American Indians account for 6.7% of the state's population. From 2016 to 2018, they made up 26% of the state's missing persons cases. [4]

Big Horn County, where I grew up, is the sixth largest county in Montana. The county which has a population of approximately 12,865 people, with Native American Indians making up for 64.8% of the population, is currently the hardest hit county in the state for this epidemic. Big Horn County has the most cases of missing and murdered in Montana. [4]

Bringing awareness to the issue has begun from within the Native American Indian communities by family members. Families whose loved ones have gone missing, or their murders are unsolved. They are raising their voices and creating change by using social media and demanding accountability of local law enforcement agencies to act and take seriously the reports when filed.

So many times, when a Native American Indian person is reported missing, it is dismissed. This is when the mothers take matters into their own hands and find themselves creating their own search parties and conducting their own investigations. Families have taken their fight against injustice to the local and federal congressional arena. They have given testimony in order to change legislative processes regarding how missing and murdered cases are handled.

Women have been for centuries the backbone of Native American Indian communities. They used to be regarded as sacred and powerful beings. A very long time ago, they were honored and respected; however, in post-Columbian times, they've been mistreated for centuries. This generational mistreatment has now escalated into an epidemic in this nation that now requires real solutions so that there comes a day when no more tears will be shed over the stolen sisters.

1. U.S. Department of Justice: Bureau of Justice Statistics. 2007 National Crime Victimization Study. 2007.
2. U.S. Department of Justice: Bureau of Justice Statistics. Rape and Sexual Assault: Reporting to Police and Medical Attention, 1992-2000, 2002
3. Department of Justice study 2016
4. Montana Department of Justice
5. National Congress of American Indians Report
6. Urban Indian Health Institute (UIHI): 2017 case studies
7. Urban Indian Health Institute: 2018 study of 71 Urban Cities Across 29 States

Matoaka

Say Her Name

Native American women have been the target of violence for centuries. One of the earliest stories told, with documentation and oral history of violence against Native American women, dates back to 1607 with a young girl named Matoaka. Her story is one that is filled with heartbreak and tragedy. However, it has been told through multi-million dollar produced Disney animated movies as a heroic love story.

Animated cartoons depict Matoaka as a young, voluptuous woman who is independent and makes decisions on her own. The truth is, she was around nine or ten years old when English settlers arrived near her village in Jamestown, Virginia. She was the daughter of the Paramount Chief of the Powhatan Chiefdom of the Mattaponi Tribe. She was raised by many aunts and other women of the tribe, as her mother had died when she was young. Matoaka was her father's favorite of all his children. She bore a resemblance to her mother whom he loved so dearly.

Captain John Smith was the man responsible for the settlement and survival of Jamestown, Virginia. After he and the English settlers became acclimated to their new surroundings in England's first permanent colony, they began to explore the outer lying areas. Twelve miles from Jamestown, they happened upon the village where Matoaka and her people lived.

In the beginning, Matoaka's tribe formed an alliance with John Smith. The two parties feared the actions of the Spanish, who had a notorious history of accelerated rivalries and conquests. Initially, Matoaka's father respected John Smith, eventually welcoming him as a leader, as John gave the tribe's people access to game and seafood.

This unification was short-lived and took an unsightly turn with the English settlers' inadequate attempts to plant crops for harvest. At that point, John Smith went to the village and demanded supplies to feed the colonists at gunpoint.

When the Europeans came to America in the early 1600s, it was a harrowing time for Native American Indian Tribes. The Native women and children wore scantily clad clothing and children often went naked. They were accustomed to wearing clothing suitable for hot, humid summers. When the white settlers arrived, the Native American Indian women and children became the targets of rape simply because the dress codes were vastly different. The white settlers viewed the Native women and young girls' lack of attire as an open invitation for sexuality.

Matoaka was coming of age in the midst of the European pilgrimage and settlement of Jamestown. Around the age of fourteen, she was considered to be transforming from a young girl to a woman. She was considered to be old enough to marry and have children of her own. A ceremony was held in which she participated in a courtship dance and chose a new name. During this ceremony, she chose the name of Pocahontas. She chose this name to commemorate her mother, who shared the same name. Her courtship dance was reserved for Kocoum. He was a younger brother of a Potowomac Chief. From this union, they had a child.

A couple of years after the birth of her first child, rumors circulated of the threat of a possible kidnapping of Pocahontas. The tribe did what they could to keep her safe. After her whereabouts were discovered and later confirmed, the settlers sent Captain Samuel Argall to get her.

The logic was that if they held a prized value, such as the daughter of a high chief, it would hamper attacks from other tribes. Captain Argall went to the village and demanded the brother of Pocahontas' husband, who was also a chief, to turn her over to them or face violence against their village. Captain Argall gave the chief a copper pot and a promise that this was just a temporary guise to defend themselves from attacks by other tribes.

In order to spare her people, Pocahontas went with the settlers. She relinquished her young son to the care of the women of the tribe. That promise, sadly, was broken. Captain Argall maintained that he had, in fact, traded Pocahontas for a copper pot.

Shortly after her abduction, she was boarded onto an English ship, completely unaware of the murder of her husband when he had gone to the village in a failed attempt to rescue her. The Powhatan tribal chiefs chose not to seek retaliation for the kidnaping of Pocahontas and the murder of her husband. They feared severe violence. They feared their reputation for being the "Peace Symbol of the Powhatan" would be tarnished.

During Pocahontas' captivity, she suffered from severe depression. She became withdrawn and very fearful. As a result, she experienced oppressive bouts of anxiety that were so severe her English captures decided to let her oldest sister and brother-in-law come to her aid. Pocahontas confided to her sister that she had been raped repeatedly.

When she became impregnated out of wedlock, she was released from captivity and was relocated to Henrico, Virginia. She gave birth to a son who was named Thomas. She was never allowed to see her child, father, or any family from her tribe.

John Rolfe was under immense pressure to meet a 1616 deadline of becoming profitable, or he would lose the support of England. He desired to learn the tobacco curing techniques from the Powhatan, who were experts. The practice was considered sacred and not to be shared with outsiders. In his attempt to politically align with the Powhatan, he decided to make Pocahontas his wife.

Prior to her marriage to John Rolfe, the settlers insisted she become "civilized," and they told her to change her ways to the English ways. They told her that her father no longer loved her because he did not come to her rescue. She was forced to dress in uncomfortable English clothes, converted to Christianity, and renamed Rebecca.

It is suspected that she was forced into a marriage with John Rolfe strictly as a means for him to gain political strength with the tribe. It is unclear if she learned to love him. It is important to know that not only did her father not attend the wedding, but he also did not partake in the traditional honor of giving his daughter away at her wedding ceremony to her new husband.

He feared that his presence would be misconstrued as an act of trying to rescue her and result in an outcome of being murdered like her first husband. Instead, he sent her a gift of a strand of pearls which were obtained from the Chesapeake Bay oyster beds and were quite large.

John Rolfe eventually ended up taking Pocahontas, now only being referred to as Rebecca, her son Thomas, her captor Captain Samuel Argall, and several Native tribal members, including her sister, back to England. He wanted to show the English elite the friendships they created with the Native Nations in order to gain acceptance and obtain continued financial support for the settlers.

After Pocahontas' grand display to the English elites, she was in a better position to express herself as she gained acceptance by the English. They did not approve of the mistreatment by the settlers. She met up with John Smith and expressed to him her outrage at his use of power to mistreat her people.

She desperately yearned to return home with the hope of reuniting with her first-born son and her father. Plans were made for her return to Virginia in the spring of 1617. According to her sister, Pocahontas was in good health in England and on the ship, preparing to return home. One evening during her voyage home after dining with her husband and Captain Argall, she vomited uncontrollably and violently. She died suddenly, leading to the belief that she had been poisoned.

She was twenty-one years old at the time of her death. Instead of being returned home to America, laid to rest with her family members and given a traditional burial by her people, she was taken to Gravesend, England. She was buried at Saint George's Church, where a monument was placed in her honor. Virginia tribes asked for the return of her remains to her homeland, but officials in England claim that the exact whereabouts of her remains are unknown.

Big Horn County, Montana

I grew up in Big Horn County, Montana, in the county seat of the predominately white town of Hardin. Big Horn County is located in the south east corner of the state. It is the home of the Hardin Bulldogs, Lodge Grass Indians, and the Plenty Coup Warriors. Census records show the county population in 2016 was 13, 563 with 28% of those living in the towns and 72% living in the rural areas. It was founded in 1913 and has a total land area of 5,015 square miles. 4995 of that is land, and 19 square miles is water.

Big Horn Country is the fifth largest county in Montana, and most of the county's land is Indian Reservations. The Crow Indian Reservation covers 64.2% of the county. The Northern Cheyenne Indian Reservation covers 6.37% of the county, leaving 29.43% as non-tribal lands. According to the US Census of 2010, the racial make-up of Big Horn County is 64.3% American Indian, 31.4% white, 2.6% two or more races, 0.5% Asian, and 0.2% African American.

According to data collected by Big Horn County between 2016 and 2019, about 23.3% of the people residing in Big Horn County live below the poverty line. The percentage of people living below the poverty line for the entire state of Montana is 12.5%. Native American Indian residents make up one-quarter of the state's average for living below the poverty line. These census numbers make sense to me. Growing up, I saw more families, including my own, just getting by than there were families that got ahead.

My family moved to Big Horn County, MT, when I was four years old. We moved there as my father accepted a job managing a well-known restaurant in the state. He was a hot commodity in the restaurant business in town. He managed, owned, and worked for several restaurants until he was diagnosed with a heart condition that kept him from working in a high-stress kitchen.

When I think back to my days of growing up in Big Horn County, I mostly think of basketball, Crow Fair, Little Big Horn Battlefield, and Yellowtail Dam at Big Horn Canyon National Recreation Area. I remember cold, snowy winters and dry, hot summers. I remember driving long distances from Hardin with my dad to go fishing on the Big Horn River and also spending time in the Big Horn Canyon. I wasn't much into fishing. I mostly lost the lures and caught no fish. I was much more interested in catching a tan than a fish.

My childhood friend's father took us fishing and boating in that same area many times. Since he was Native American Indian, he had more access to certain parts of the river and the dam. I thought it was super cool. My friend had the lightest white complexion of any of my friends. Everyone was always surprised when they found out her dad was a full-blooded Native American Indian.

He worked for the BIA, and he was very much a light-hearted man. I think I was a little envious she had such a cool dad. I liked to hang out with her family because they had a real sense of family unity. It's not that I didn't have a good, cohesive family; it's just their family was different.

As kids, we all think our friend's parents are cooler and better than the ones we have and take for granted. Family is important on the reservation and within Indian country. Even people that aren't blood-related become family. Families are close-knit. Traditionally, Native American Indians are people collectors in the sense that if friends or acquaintances visit your house, the minute they walk through the threshold, they become family.

Across the street from where I lived was a house that we could never keep track of who lived there. The primary home owner was a Native Indian woman who had a good reputation in town. She was a nice lady. She held a good job in town. She took care of her family no matter what their situation. I'm not even sure some of the people who lived in her house, even if for the short term, were actually blood-related. That didn't matter. As long as they were under her roof, they were family.

There were two small boys who lived in that house, and they were over at our house every day, almost all day long. My younger brother was close to their age. They came over to be with our small little family for companionship and presumably escape whatever adult situations were going on in their house. They were adorable little boys. I still think of them and what's become of them. While they were at our house, they were part of our family.

We lived on the corner of the street, located pretty centrally in town. I was never too far from anyplace that I couldn't walk to get to. I walked to school every day. If I timed it right, I could escape total embarrassment in front of my friends by avoiding my dad giving me a ride to school. I tried to plan it so that I would arrive at the exact location of one of the hottest guys in school who also was walking to school. Walking through the high school doors with him by my side gave me some incredible cool points with my fellow schoolmates.

Much to my disappointment, he never asked me out. He was a super nice guy and very popular. Most of the girls had a crush on him, but he wasn't one who dated much. You didn't see him in the hallways kissing and making out with anyone. He didn't have the weekly hickeys on his neck that were indications that this boy (or girl) was taken and belonged to someone. Since he had no girlfriend, I could safely walk through the doors of my high school with him without the fear of getting beat up by a jealous girlfriend.

There are four levels of school in Hardin. The Primary School is grades K-3. The Elementary School which is grades 4-6. The Junior High School includes grades 7-8, and the High School includes grades 9-12. Most of the kids I graduated with I knew since kindergarten.

In Junior High, the class size grew as we picked up the kids who had lived outside of town. They attended grades K-6 at small country schools. We also picked up some kids from the reservation.

In High School, we picked up even more kids from the reservation. The small rural schools only went as high as 8th grade. I would say that my High School was at least half White students and the other half Native American Indian.

In primary and elementary school, it was usually the white boys who would scuffle on the playground. Most fights were to show who was the toughest or to prove they didn't have a crush on a girl. When we entered Junior High and our class grew, the fighting switched from just the white boys to the Native

American Indian girls. I remember there being more knock-down, drag-out, hair-pulling, fingernail-scratching fights between the Native American girls.

By High School, the fights were taken away from the school grounds and out of everyone's sight. Everyone knew who got into a fight as they'd show up for class the next morning with a black eye to prove it. You always wanted to be on good terms with the tough girls who won the fights she got into.

Summers in Big Horn County brought summer camp, the carnival, the rodeo, the circus, the Crow Fair, and migrant workers. All of these things were the outlets of escape from the dull drums of small-town life. It never failed that at least a few girls professed they were in love for the first time with a carnie worker, someone from another tribe, or a migrant worker who was just there for summer work.

Winters brought about hardships, blizzards, boredom, but most importantly, winter high school sports. One thing that almost everyone would agree upon in Big Horn County is that basketball keeps the community together. It's like the heartbeat and brings the people in the county together. The excitement and energy in the high school gymnasium at a game is astounding.

It's almost like the basketball has a soul of its own. When it is profoundly quiet, you can hear the echo of the ball dribbling on the hardwood floor. You can hear the swoosh sound when the ball touches nothing but the net. When it's loud, it's very, very loud. Everyone goes to the games, and the gymnasium is usually so packed that it becomes standing-room only.

Everyone wants a winning team, and the team is always chasing down that state championship trophy. In the spring of

2020, just before the shut-downs from the pandemic, the county's basketball teams won three state championship basketball titles. The Hardin boys' varsity basketball team, the Hardin girls' varsity basketball team, and the Lodge Grass boys' varsity basketball team all brought home the coveted title of being state champions. The Native Indians are athletes by nature. Both the native boys and girls start playing basketball at a very young age.

After high school, if they aren't awarded scholarships, they still remain athletic by being involved in the rodeo. One of my friends from elementary school operates the championship Indian Relay Horse Racing team. He is a very active member of the rodeo and the community.

Every year during Crow Fair and all summer long, the best place to find him is at the horse track and the rodeo grounds. Indian Relay Horse Racing is a relatively new sport. It is a pretty incredible sight to behold. The first time I saw a live Indian Relay Horse Race, I was completely blown away. These races are a true form of absolute athleticism like I've never seen before.

Even though Big Horn County, where there is a sense of family unity, outdoor recreation, and amazing athletes, there is something darker that lurks in the shadows of the night under the big skies of Montana. Big Horn County is currently considered the most dangerous county for a young Native American Indian woman to live in. According to The Sovereign Bodies Institute, at least thirty-two women have gone missing or have been murdered in Big Horn County since 1977, which is more than any other county in Montana. At least half of all Missing and Murdered Indigenous People's cases have gone unsolved.

The Sovereign Bodies Institute reports that twenty-six of those cases have happened in the last 20 years. In addition to the women having been reported as missing or murdered, there have been 19 reported cases of men who have gone missing or been murdered in Big Horn County as well. Their families are seeking answers and justice for the unnecessary deaths of their children.

Troy Small

Say His Name

<u>May 3, 1972 – February 11, 2008</u>

A Cheyenne Prayer

Let us walk together,

Do not walk in front of me,

I may not follow, and; I may not lead,

But let us walk together,

In good fellowship and

Together we will reach our common goal.

By Frank Walksabout

"Why don't you come to the Kirby Saloon with me?" Troy's mother asked him as they stood in the doorway of his trailer at their ranch home.

"Nah, mom. I've got lots of work to do around here." He replied as he looked around at the work that needed to be done.

"You need to be taking it easy and let those broken ribs heal, son."

"Mom, I'm fine. Really, I am. I'm getting stronger every day."

"Well, you should still be letting people help you out more for a while." She pleaded with him one last time to join her.

"Go mom. Enjoy your dinner and tell my big brother, I'll save some work for him to do, so he'd better eat a big meal."

"Do you want me to bring something back for you?"

"You're such a great mom. I'm good. I've got lots to eat here. Go on now, Shane's probably wondering where the heck you are." He looked at his watch, hinting to her that she was running late by doting on him. "Love you, mom."

She placed the palm of her hand on his cheek. "Love you too, son. I just wish you wouldn't work so hard. You are so damn stubborn sometimes."

She turned around and walked to her car. He waved to her as she slowly drove away.

Troy looked around the ranch and saw the large stack of cinder blocks that needed to be moved. There was no way he was going to be able to lift them without help due to his broken ribs. He was still unable to lift heavy objects without it causing him some pain. Everyone was telling him to take it easy, but he just wanted to get back to being himself without restrictions. He decided he'd just do some minor cleaning up and then call it a night.

He stood in the doorway of his mobile home and wiped his brow. He was thinking of getting himself an iced cold drink when suddenly he was looking his killer in the face. He felt the cold steel blade of the knife slice through his skin. He felt the instant pain and shock as it pierced his chest, just missing his heart. The killer retracted the blade as Troy grabbed his chest. As he gasped for a breath, he felt another piercing blow to his chest. Once again, it just missed his heart.

As the knife was retracted a second time, blood poured out of the open wounds. Troy dropped to his knees in agony. His adrenaline was rushing, and he was in a fight for his life. With hopes that the killer would stop, he felt the hot blood-soaked blade turn attention to his neck. A couple of slashes were made on his neck. The final slash that ended his life was to the jugular vein in his neck.

Troy fell to the ground, gasping for air, as he put his hands to his throat to stop the flow of blood gushing to the ground. But it was just too immense, and he died on the porch of his trailer from the blood loss. He took his last breaths with the intent of surviving and identifying his killer.

Shane Small was waiting for his mother to arrive at the Kirby Saloon. She had just left the Small's ranch to meet him for dinner and to catch up on all the latest news going on in his life.

"Shane, it's so good to see you," his mother said as she greeted her son inside the Kirby Saloon. He'd already had a table and menus waiting for three people.

"It's good to see you too, Ma. Where's Troy?" Shane asked.

"He's not coming. He said he had to get some things done yet at the ranch. You know him, always the hard worker and all. I tried to get him to come. Really, I did."

"Is he taking it easy with his broken ribs?" Shane inquired. "I still can't believe he tipped his motorcycle."

"He's lucky all he did was crack some ribs, and of course he's not. You know your brother. Nothing slows him down. Even though he can't lift much right now, he's still working away. It's probably why it's taking him more time to get things done right now. I asked him if he needed more help around there until he's fully mended." His mother replied.

The two made a small conversation and looked at the menus. A woman sitting in the saloon who worked at the nearby hospital in Busby received a phone call.

"Hello," she answered. "Oh my, yes, I'll be there right away." She immediately got up to leave.

Shane and his mother looked at her. "Everything Okay?" they asked her.

"No, there's a DOA up at Kirby."

Shane felt a knot in the pit of his stomach. He knew it was his brother.

"Mom, we've got to go now! I think it's Troy."

"What makes you think that? I just saw him. It can't be," she said with a nervous tone.

"I just know." Shane replied.

They grabbed their coats, laid money on the table for their tab and rushed out of the saloon. They jumped into Shane's car and rushed towards the ranch. When Shane and his mother rounded the last corner of the road, arriving at Troy's ranch, they saw the red and blue police and ambulance lights lighting up the night sky. Shane abruptly ran out of his car to the ambulance. He saw his dad sitting upright in the back of the ambulance. He was relieved to see his dad was okay. He was still trying to figure out what exactly was going on.

"Dad! Dad!" Shane screamed. "What the hell is going on?"

Shane's dad did not reply. He just hung his head in sorrow. Shane frantically ran to Troy's trailer that was on the property. He was stopped at gunpoint.

"I'm sorry Shane," one of the officers said, "It's Troy."

"He's gone, isn't he?" Shane cried out.

The officer nodded.

As previously mentioned, it isn't just the women who go missing or are murdered in Big Horn County. The men also fall victim to senseless deaths. Troy Small is one of those tragic stories about a life cut short too soon. A life cut short for no good reason. There were no big story headlines in the newspapers about his death. He became just another statistic of domestic violence. His story was never told.

Searching the archives of the newspapers, all you will find is his obituary, leaving out the cause of death. I, myself, hadn't realized that his untimely death should be categorized under unsolved cases of Big Horn County until I started researching and talking to Shane.

Troy worked on his family's ranch. The ranch was his livelihood and passion. Even as a kid, Troy had a love for the family ranch. Family members who spent time with Troy as kids recall such fond memories of him and his brothers. His favorite activities were mechanic work, snowmobiling, and four-wheeling. He loved the rodeo, and he was good at it. A natural, so to speak.

He is described as a guy who was level-headed and quick to make a joke and laugh with everyone. He had many friends. He was friends with just about everyone. Some of his friends he referred to as family. He was loyal to those he knew and loved.

He was the kind of guy who could find the humor in almost any situation. He was known for making everyone smile, even if they were sad or upset.

It's difficult to find a person who didn't like Troy or had anything negative to say about him. He is deeply missed by his family, children, and friends. His brother Shane tells me that his brother was murdered and that his death still devastates and haunts him to this day. Every year on February 11, Shane relives the horrible day of his brother's death like it just happened.

When Shane opened up to me about what transpired after his brother's murder, he told me a story that is told by many in Big Horn County. A story of an investigation that was incredibly lacking. He felt embarrassed for the way the BIA, the FBI, and the Criminal Investigators were behaving at the crime scene.

After the county coroner came and took Troy's body, everyone else left, too. Everyone. Just gone. They left the family in the main house to make sense of it all. They left Troy's trailer house door wide open and left the crime scene completely unsecure. No crime tape was put up. None of the family was questioned by authorities that night.

The family feels that the investigators probing Troy's death asked very few questions. They didn't write down information the family felt was most important. On the evening of Troy's death, two people living on the property witnessed a dark blue van leaving the ranch at a high rate of speed. The driver almost collided into the front gate of the property and nearly crashed on the highway as it disappeared into the night. The family feels not many people were questioned as to what was witnessed by others that night.

According to Shane, the knife that was used to kill Troy was never recovered. Ironically, when a remodeling project was taking place at the ranch in 2017, one of the ranch hands found a knife coated in blood. It was stashed in an eave that contained a hole. The ranch hand was surprised by the find. Not knowing what to do, he put the knife back exactly where he found it. A few hours later, he informed Shane of what he found. Shane promptly went to look for the knife, but when he frantically searched for the lethal weapon, it was not there.

Shane tells me he felt like his family was treated like they were criminals. He was questioned by the Feds at midnight when everyone was in bed. He opened up to them and told them what he suspected happened. He felt his words fell on deaf ears.

Shane was jailed by authorities a day or two after his brother's death. Not for committing a crime of any kind. The reason given to him was authorities thought he was going to retaliate and seek vengeance for the murder of his brother. The family has tried to come forward with information to help solve the mystery of his death. They want to prove that he was indeed the victim of a senseless crime and not a cruel monster deserving death as a way of an end to a means of domestic violence.

The main person the family suspects killed Troy didn't spend any time in jail. A woman was arrested on tribal charges but was soon released as she told investigators that she stabbed Troy in self-defense. She claimed it was self-defense. She claimed he was threatening to hit her with a forty-pound cinderblock.

Shane has remained strong in his belief that the excuse of self-defense was a fabricated story in order to protect another person from being charged with committing a cold-blooded, pre-meditated murder. The person who the family suspects murdered Troy was found dead on his kitchen floor in the fall of 2012. To this day, twelve years later, no one has been charged in Troy's murder.

Jack Daniels, Mary Jane, and Friends

᠃

Growing up, I was exposed to witnessing the effects of what alcohol does to a person. My father managed and cooked for a few restaurants in Hardin, MT. A couple of them were on Skid Row and connected to a bar. As a kid, I would sit in the kitchen on a five-gallon pickle bucket, eat pickles to my heart's content, and observe. I remember clearly one of his patrons would come stumbling into the restaurant from the bar in the afternoon. He always asked for a raw hamburger.

My Dad would serve it to him for free as every time he tried to cook it, the patron got mad. "I said raw, God Damn it!" He'd shout.

My Dad would tell him, "Ok, fine, but watch your language, or you're out of here."

This man enjoyed eating raw hamburgers whenever he was highly intoxicated. Not only did he enjoy it, he demanded it be raw. Not cooked at all. He took pleasure in consuming the frigid limp meat patty as the blood would soak through the bun and drip down his chin onto the plate.

My Dad wasn't the only business who would look away when it came to alcoholism and the alcoholics that roamed around town. The local library was a spot where they would also congregate to attempt to sober up or as a spot to continue chasing the high. They would sometimes sleep on the lawn beneath the big oak trees that provided shade. They would go to the library, and depending on who was on shift, they could take a nap in one of the big, comfy reclining chairs.

Sometimes, when I walked down Skid Row (the part of town where all the bars were located side by side up and down the street), I would be approached by drunken people for money. Of course, at eight years old, this was sometimes frightening. By being exposed to it so many times, I learned who they were. They were always totally harmless.

They were just people out of sorts turning to alcohol to try to absolve them of their problems or whatever demons they were fighting. I was never allowed at the restaurant at night as my mother always said, "Nothing good ever happens after midnight."

Night time on skid row was when the adults drank. Fights would break out between the different factions of natives, rail road crew, seismographers, and miners.

At that time in town, alcohol, marijuana, and Lysol were the drugs of choice. In 3rd grade, my class toured the county jail. On our tour, we got to see the evidence room. I had never seen so much marijuana in all my life. At the time, I had no idea what it was. All I knew was that there were a whole lot of drugs they had confiscated.

I was in a group called Camp Fire Girls growing up. It was an afterschool program for girls from first to twelfth grade. A couple times a year we would all come together and clean up the town. We called it Operation Sparkle. We cleaned up the trash around town.

There was one lot that was notoriously known for where the Lysol huffers got high. It was a rocky lot next to the grocery store on the outskirts of town that was overgrown with tall weeds. It provided a safe haven for Lysol huffers. They weren't easy to see amongst the overgrown weeds.

We cleaned up this lot on several occasions. Amongst the numerous empty beer cans, there were empty cans of Lysol aerosol. It took me a long time to figure out why there were always so many empty cans of Lysol until someone told me. Occasionally, while cleaning up, we'd run across someone who was passed out lying amongst beer bottles and empty Lysol cans. We would just leave them be and not disturb them.

There was a man who lived for at time in the house with the revolving door of people across the street from me. Every time I saw him, it was evident he was highly intoxicated. He would always cut across our front yard as he made his way to Skid Row for his next fix.

One day, my dad had enough of him cutting through our yard, so he decided to build a wooden fence. Not a large one, just a simple wooden fence to keep him from cutting across and forcing him to use the sidewalk. The day that my dad and I were out getting ready to put up this fence, the man came stumbling from his house across the street onto our property. He wanted to know what was going on.

"Well, I'm building a fence to keep you from cutting across my front yard all the time," my dad told him. The man thought that was a swell idea. He even asked if he could help. He needed some money. So, my dad put him to work. My dad gave him a shovel. He instructed him where and how to dig the holes so we could put the fence posts in.

That afternoon, he dug nine semi-perfect fence post holes in our yard. My dad paid him one dollar for each hole. He walked away with nine dollars in his pocket, and was the happiest man in the world. That day, he wouldn't have to beg or plead people for money to pay for his alcohol habit. You would have thought he won the lottery. He was the richest poor man that day.

But alas, the money did run out, as we all suspected. Hours later, he came knocking on our door. He smelled of booze and asked if we had more holes for him to dig. Unfortunately, we did not. His job was done. He said Ok, and left.

Deep down, he was not a bad man. Maybe that afternoon of digging holes gave him a glimmer of hope for the man he could be. Sadly, he was someone who gave into the bottle. He let it take over and consume him. I never knew what his story was, but I think it would be safe to say it was most likely littered with tragedy and heartache.

Alcoholism and substance abuse have been a big problem on reservations, not just in Big Horn County but in other reservations as well. Although the use of drugs, alcohol, and substance abuse vary from tribe to tribe, it is one of the biggest sources of health problems facing Native American Indians. The U.S. Indian Health Service has cited alcohol, tobacco, and chemical substances as an urgent health problem.

The National Institute of Health conducted studies that show there is evidence for the inheritability of alcohol and drug dependence. They compared a few tribes and found links in their genetic chromosomal components of metabolizing enzyme variants. They found that the tribes they studied had some differences. They found that the Native American Indians' socio-culture, environmental factors (such as poverty, lack of health care, generational abuse, and other factors), along with genetics, are predisposed to become addicts at higher rates than any other ethnicity.

Numerous studies conducted by the National Institute of Health show that people who experience trauma, live in poverty, have broken homes, have low levels of education, and other such adversities are more likely to use and abuse alcohol and drugs than people who have a better socioeconomic status.

Most reservations around America are dry. This was a requirement to obtain tribal lands by early US governing authorities. At the time, white people thought Indians couldn't handle "the fire water."

Becoming a wet reservation takes an act of congress to make happen. Although some reservations have gone wet without issue, it does affect the tribe's sovereignty claims. Going from dry to wet certainly doesn't change the state of affairs that exists on reservations. Even though the Crow and the Northern Cheyenne reservations are both dry reservations, just like during the prohibition, it doesn't stop anyone from obtaining alcohol and getting drunk. It's almost like it makes it more appealing.

The bars off the reservation closest to the boundary lines are the Kirby Saloon and Jimtown. During daylight hours, both are fine establishments. After the sun goes down, they both have a reputation for having a rough-and-tumble tough crowd. Both are small establishments with a down-home country feel to them. Back in the day, the barstools at Jimtown were nailed to the floor to keep the patrons from throwing them around during a bar brawl. Now, they've been replaced with very heavy tree stump-like seats. You'd have to be Paul Bunyan to pick one of them up.

It isn't just alcohol problems that afflict the residents of the reservations. Substance abuse is also very prevalent. From the 1960s to the 1980s, marijuana was the biggest drug of choice. That is until heroin and meth made its way to reservation territory.

With heroine becoming cheaper than marijuana, it's easy to understand why this drug has taken the place of marijuana.

Reservations aren't the only places plagued with an addiction to this drug.

Meth, on the other hand, has now taken over. It's easy to get, cheap, and easy to make. Anyone can make it. People have now found a way to make it in an empty water bottle, which does not include having to cook it down. Meth makers believe this eliminates the dangers of having a catastrophic meth cooking mishap.

Methamphetamine is a synthetic man-made drug commonly concocted in discrete hidden locations. Mixing various forms of amphetamine or derivatives with other chemicals, such as battery acid, drain cleaner, lantern fuel, ammonia hydroxide, and antifreeze, is why the making of meth is so dangerous. Sometimes, when the cooks are too high and don't have their wits about them, the kitchen will explode, leaving them severely burned or even killed.

The additives of meth are highly toxic. The production of one pound of meth produces five pounds of waste. This waste is very dangerous. People exposed to the waste will experience symptoms of being poisoned. Storage of highly toxic chemicals is also very dangerous, as the chemicals can seep into items it is stored near, such as clothing or food.

I spoke with several people about drugs on the reservation. They all pointed to meth. I asked where it came from. They informed me that it comes from I-90, the main freeway artery through Montana. They told me the cartel brings it in, and it's just simply easy to make. You don't have to look too far to get it.

I'm told by locals that women in Big Horn County and on the reservation are the biggest users of meth. I'm not sure what the actual statistics are of men versus women using meth, but certainly, the perception in Big Horn County is that women are the ones who are most afflicted with meth addiction. It's introduced by someone they know, love, and trust at an early age. The perception is that the age of introduction is getting younger and younger.

Meth use has become a huge problem on reservations. In 2016 The Fort Belknap reservation, located in the upper northern plains of Montana, declared a "state of emergency" based on a resurgence of meth use and arrests after a decline about ten years earlier. Since then, a few other tribes across the nation have since declared similar "states of emergency" to combat the meth problem and the problems it brings to the reservations.

Many tribal members are at a loss as to what to do. They see their people become slaves to addiction to this dangerous drug. Labeled as "zombies" by locals, meth turns its subjects into fidgety, skinny shells of a person. Severe meth addicts are easy to spot, as they've let the sense of proper hygiene go by the wayside. They have large, dilated eyes, and they have a certain twitch to them.

It's a sad, helpless path to go down. People are turned onto the drug out of boredom, curiosity, and weight control. Some become addicts to numb the pain and forget about the things happening around them that they have no control over.

People who have become addicted to meth usually have common stories. They were pressured by peers. They were told it was no big deal. The reality is that meth is so highly addictive that users become addicted after just one single use. Meth makes the user feel like they have super human powers. It numbs the pain.

Users share similar stories when they realize they have a problem with the drug. It begins with, "I was arrested and thrown in jail." It ends with "I lost everything". Losses of their homes, their earthly possessions, extending to losing their children and loved ones. You'll hear stories of "I sold someone else's (often times a close family member, a mother, a father, a child, an aunt, and an uncle) item of high value. They may have even begged their closest friends for money.

If they've escaped meth addiction with their life, that's a feat in itself. Ex-meth addicts often have a problem with relapse. Just like any other drug, hanging out with the people who brought them into addiction ends up dragging addicts right back in. The only way for them to really kick the habit is to not have contact with people they hung out with and brought them into their addiction.

In rural Montana, that's a difficult task. Users and recovered addicts find themselves moving from town to town, trying to find a job with a criminal record. They try to piece back the pieces of their lives, which are often times in complete ruins. To hear a meth addict survivor's story is very moving, as you will hear them talk about putting their lives back together. They try to move on with severe losses and felony criminal records hanging over their heads. They, just like any other ex-addict, have the daily struggle to fight that addiction and the actions of their past that haunt them.

I scoured the newspaper archives and found many articles about meth seizures that have happened throughout the last thirty years. Meth bust after meth bust after meth bust, all headed for the big sky country, adding up to millions in dollars of street value.

I would read "the biggest meth drug bust in Montana history" in one newspaper article and then see another article a few years later with the same headline." It seems as though it's a never-ending funneling of meth into Montana, coming from as far as Mexico and Florida, hidden in fruits and vegetables, car paneling, stuffed toys, pillow cases, and even disguised as children's vitamins headed right to easy prey… the reservation.

Roylynn Louise Rides Horse

Say Her Name

January 8, 1988 – June 28, 2016

But they that wait upon the Lord shall renew their strength;
they shall mount up with the wings as eagles; they shall run,
and not be weary; and they shall walk, and not be faint.

Isaiah 40:31

Roylynn's phone was ringing. With a child in her arms, she searched for her ringing phone. It was located underneath a pile of the kids' clothes that she had just laundered and folded. She answered right before it quit ringing. Her caller ID indicated it was her mother calling.

"Hi, Ma," Roylynn said as she jostled the phone between her ear and her shoulder. She rebalanced her child on her hip. One of her other children in the background jumped up and down. "Is that grandma?!" Her young son asked with glee.

"Yes honey, its grandma. I told you we're seeing her tomorrow." Her son scurried away, excited that he was going to get to spend time with Grandma the next day.

"Lynnie Girl," her mother said, "why don't you and the kids come to Billings with me tomorrow? I'll take you all shopping. Then I'll take you all out to eat. The kids will have fun, and it'll be good for you, too."

"Ma, I'd love to go, but between the move and everything else going on," her voice drifted for a moment, "plus, I'm going to see if my man will take me on a date. It's been a while, and things have been crazy."

"Come on, Lynnie Girl," her mother pleaded, "he can go out with you another night."

"Ma, I know you don't like him, but he's not a bad guy. I'll go to Billings with you another time." She responded.

"Lynnie Girl quit fooling yourself. You're too good for him." her mom stated.

"Ma, let's not start this. Things are just crazy. I do appreciate you taking the kids tomorrow, though." Roylynn emphatically stated.

"I'm telling you, he's no good for you. He's too controlling of you. I don't like that." She wasn't going to let it go.

"I love you too, Ma." Roylynn said, "I'll bring the kids over tomorrow. You can take them to Billings if you want; I'm sure they'd love that. They are excited to see you. Muah!" She pretended to give her mom a big kiss as she hung up the phone. She continued preparing her kids' belongings so she could drop them off with her mom the next day.

The next day, she gathered up the kids' belongings she had gathered the night before, packed up the kids in the car, and drove them to her mom's house. Roylynn's mom greeted the children on the front door step. The kids clamored out of the car, excitedly running in to see their grandma. They raced each other for the first cookie they knew was waiting for them. This was always the case when they visited their grandma.

Roylynn stayed by the car. She did not follow the children but rather waved at her mom while leaning against the car.

"Thanks, Ma!" she shouted as she blew her a kiss from where she stood. She didn't dare go in. Her mom would try to talk her into a trip to Billings. She wasn't in the mood to have that conversation again. She'd made up her mind.

She got back into her car and drove away from her mother's house. She glanced into her rear-view mirror as she drove away. She headed home to wait for her boyfriend to get off work and then go out. She was going to spend the evening with her man. Just the two of them alone for once.

"Would you like me to fix you a drink before we head out?" he asked Roylynn.

"Ah, sure, babe, that'd be great. I'm almost ready to go." Roylynn replied with a smile. She was excited to be spending a date night out. It had been a while since the two of them had gone out together.

"Here you go, my dear." He said as he handed her a drink and gave her a quick kiss on the cheek. "You look beautiful."

"Thanks, hon." She blushed. It'd been a while since he told her she was beautiful. Maybe this was a sign that he was loosening up on his suspicions of her cheating. "Ha!" she thought to herself, "like when do I have time to cheat? With six kids, I'm too busy to be stepping out on anyone."

She gave him a smile and took a sip of the drink he'd made for her. "Mmm… now that's my kind of bar tender." She said as she let the drink quench her freshly glossed lips.

They finished their drinks and left the house holding hands. They got in the car and drove to the Kirby Saloon. When they arrived, they sat at the bar and ordered a drink. One drink turned into two, turned into three, and so on. She tried to make small talk with her boyfriend, but he seemed distant. His eyes gazed off beyond what Roylynn was talking about or doing.

Roylynn was a bit disgusted that he didn't seem to be paying attention to her. She felt her words were falling upon deaf ears. She got up from her barstool to take part in the line dance that was happening in the center of the bar. Her boyfriend sat at the bar watching as she moved her body back and forth to the music along with the crowd. She was smiling and having a good time. When the dance was over, she joined her boyfriend back at the bar, but he was furious. "What the hell was that all about?" He sneered.

"What was what about?" she gave him a puzzled look. Things had been going fine, and now, suddenly, he's in a bad mood. "You mean that?" She inquired as she pointed at the dance floor. "That was line dancing. Relax, ain't no big thing for you to get all worked up about."

"Yeah, what was that? You were shaking your ass all for all the guys here to drool over and wanting to snag my woman." He replied.

"Oh my God! You've got to be kidding me. One-line dance, and now I'm some kind of slut or what? Wow, just wow." She picked up her drink and turned away. She took a giant gulp. She slammed her glass on the bar, looked at the bar tender, tapped her finger on the edge of the glass, and said, "Hit me up, just one more."

"Just admit it; you'd leave with anyone of these guys here." He said.

"Are you kidding me right now? You've got to be joking. I've never cheated. I would never cheat on you." She replied angrily. "Running around on you? How the hell am I gonna run around on you when I'm taking care of my six kids? You think I have time to run around? Quit being dramatic, and lets to try to enjoy our night together. Remember, I chose a night out with you over going with my mom and the kids to Billings."

She continued, "If anything, you are the one I should be worried about. I've had a feeling you've been out snagging around, but I thought maybe, just maybe, that wasn't true since you decided to take me out, but now the way you are acting all jealous, I'm really beginning to wonder if maybe it's you that's the one stepping out."

Roylynn had had some suspicions. She had no proof, but she had a gut feeling. A woman's intuition. She knew he was the jealous type, but he was being ridiculous at that moment. They continued to argue some more and exchanged heated words.

Finally, he'd heard all he could for the night. "That's it, I'm leaving! Your ass can find its own way home tonight. I oughta throw all your shit out before you get home."

He got off the barstool, pulled the keys from his pocket, and left the bar. He left Roylynn behind, standing at the bar completely dumbfounded as to what had just transpired. She ran after him, but it was too late. He drove away before she could stop him. She went back into the bar, sat down, ordered another drink, and tried to hold back the tears that started to fall down her cheeks.

As Roylynn sat alone, struggling to fight back the tears, a woman in the bar approached her. It was Angelica Whiteman. "Hey, what's up?" Angelica said as she approached Roylynn.

"Nothing that concerns you," Roylynn replied.

"You sure about that?"

"Yeah, I'm fine. Not looking for company right now."

"Fine if you say so, but those tears say otherwise, sister."

"Really, I'm fine; I just want to be alone."

Angelica left and went back to the table of people she was drinking with.

Roylynn looked around the bar, realizing that she was stranded there with no way home. She grabbed her purse and searched for her phone. It wasn't there. She searched frantically, dumping the entire contents of her purse on the bar top. Her phone was not there. She panicked and ran her hands through everything on the bar and spread it out. There was no phone.

"Oh great!" She muttered. She tried to retrace her steps in her mind as to where her phone might be. She either left it at home, or it fell out of her purse in the car on their way over to the bar. Either way, she was definitely stranded with no contacts as those were all in her phone. She didn't have anyone's number but her own memorized. She didn't have them written down anywhere, either.

She glanced around some more, wondering which one of these lucky patrons would be the lucky winner of being her free taxi for the night. She figured she would approach Angelica. Angelica made contact with her, and Roylynn brushed her off. She hoped she would be forgiving.

"Hey, so I kind of need a ride home and was wondering if you guys could be so kind to oblige." She asked as she sucked up her pride and bit her lower lip just a bit.

"Thought you didn't need any company," Angelica said quizzically.

"Yeah, well, I guess I do after all. I mean, if it's not too much. I need a ride home. So, yeah, I guess I could use a friend right about now." She replied.

"Sure, no problem," Angelica said, "have a drink with us, and then we'll go. Come on, let's go get one last drink, and I'm gonna grab a few bottles for the road home."

Roylynn followed Angelica to the bar; they ordered a drink. The ladies raised their glasses to each other, clinked them together gently, gulped it quickly, and then set their empty glasses on the bar. They smiled at one another. Angelica nodded at the group she was with and motioned to them that it was time to leave.

"Which way you headed?" Angelica asked Roylynn.

"Can you take me to my mom's place in Crow?" she asked.

"Sure, but we were kind of headed the other way. You sure you don't know anybody in our general direction." Angelica responded as they all walked out of the bar towards the car.

"Nah, take me to Crow. "She said as she got in the back seat of the car. Angelica jumped into the front passenger seat in front of Roylynn. She opened a bottle of beer and took a sip. The others got into the car, and they drove off. It was a bit of a drive. The two women began to argue about Roylynn's boyfriend.

"How do you know my boyfriend?" Roylynn asked.

"Girl, he's been snagging my best friend for a long time," Angelica replied.

"That's not true. Why would you say something like that?" Roylynn replied

"Believe it. He only went out with you tonight cuz she was busy. He's gonna dump your ass for her. Time to face facts."

The two girls continued to argue. Finally, Angelica lost her temper. She turned around and began punching Roylynn. Roylynn didn't see the attack coming, and she fought back, but Angelica had an advantage as she was throwing punches while leaning over the front seat on top of Roylynn.

"What the hell bitch?" Roylynn shouted as she tried to kick and punch Angelica off of her.

"I'm a mess you up bitch!" Angelica proclaimed as she continued to throw punches to Roylynn's face.

Angelica leaned over further. She took a beer bottle and smashed it over Roylynn's head. Then she started to choke Roylynn. Roylynn did everything she could to fight back. Her body went limp in the back seat after Angelica delivered a sucker punch to her face.

"Shit," she said as she looked at Roylynn's slumped body in the back seat of the car, "we gotta take care of this bitch. Turn down that road up ahead. We gotta get rid of her." She instructed the driver, Dimarzio Sanchez, as she pointed to Castle Rock Road.

Dimarzio turned and drove down Castle Rock Road a little bit before he stopped. He put the car in park and looked at Angelica in puzzlement. Angelica kicked open the front door and swung the back door of the car open. She grabbed Roylynn by the hair and dragged her out of the back seat onto the ground. Roylynn started to come to and started to fight back.

Angelica instructed a couple of the passengers in the car to get back in the vehicle and turn the music up while two of the men and Angelica could finish working her over.

Roylynn and Angelica continued fighting. Roylynn was stripped of her clothes as Angelica continued to hit and kick Roylynn. Roylynn didn't give up; she returned a punch to Angelica that left her heading back to the car crying.

"You didn't finish it," one of the men said. Dimarzio handed Angelica a bandana and instructed her how to strangle Roylynn with it. Angelica wrapped the ends of the bandana around her hands and twisted the bandana up like a makeshift rope. She placed the bandana on Roylynn's neck and began to strangle her with it. Roylynn was weak from the beating and the alcohol. She became unable to fight back anymore. She passed out on the cold hard ground.

Angelica and Dimarizio returned to the car. He opened the trunk and took out a can of gas. He looked at the seventeen-year-old female passenger in the car, pointed his finger at her, and said to her, "Do not look back."

Angelica finished his sentence with, "If you do, you'll end up just like her."

Dimarzio carried the gas can over to the unconscious Roylynn. He poured gasoline all over her naked body. He set the gas can down, lit a match, and threw it on Roylynn's body. She burst into flames. Dimarzio and Angelica returned to the car. They drove away as they watched Roylynn's blazing body in the rear-view mirror.

Roylynn awakened and screamed in pain and horror. Her entire body was on fire. She began to roll around to put the flames out. After a bit of rolling around, she was able to extinguish the flames. She sat up with her legs stretched out in front of her. She looked at herself in horror. She took a moment to assess her bodily damage.

She was naked, in shock, in pain, and charred black from head to toe. She looked around and began to come up with a plan of survival. Her body ached, and her head was throbbing. She reached up to touch her hands to her head. She screamed when she realized she was missing so much hair. She stood up slowly as some pieces of her skin fell off around her. She looked at the dead flesh on the ground. Then she looked up and saw the lights of the town of Crow in the night skyline. The lights gave her the belief that she could make it home. It wasn't too far; she tried to convince herself. She began to walk, putting one charred foot in front of the other, slowing taking steps towards home. She knew she could make it. She just had to.

Roylynn started to walk slowly towards the lights of Crow Agency. She knew if she kept focusing on the lights, she would make it home. She wasn't going to lie down and die in the middle of nowhere. The ground was hard, cold, and uneven. The coolness felt slightly comforting, as she still felt the heat from the burns on her body. She tried not to focus on the wounds on her body, albeit difficult.

Each step was more painstaking than the next. She was determined to make it home. She took each step slowly, as the ground beneath did not give her much leeway for her aching body. After walking some distance, Roylynn found a large tree and leaned up against it. She was tired and in so much agony. She decided she would take a few moments to recollect her thoughts and strength so she could keep pushing forward.

After a few moments, she continued walking. She talked to herself the entire time, giving herself self-affirmations. She did everything she could to focus on her steps and the lights along the skyline rather than let her mind drift and flood with memories.

Afraid that she wasn't going to see her kids or at least say goodbye, she began to think of them with each painstaking step. She was determined to get back to them. Seeing their faces in her mind is what kept her going.

A few hours later, she became so weary and de-hydrated. She no longer had feeling in her toes. She tried to take another step, and it was just too much. She had walked almost three miles. She decided to sit down and rest for a while before she could continue onward. Roylynn sat down in a farmer's field. She needed to rest and regain some strength.

The night passed, and when the sun rose, Steve Peterson, a Kansas rancher with cattle in Montana, was driving around in his truck, checking on his cattle. As he was driving, he found a used straw in the cab. He opened up the back window a crack and tried to throw the straw into the bed of his truck, but it blew back into the cab. It fell behind his seat. He shut the window and continued driving.

He decided to turn down Castle Rock Road in order to relieve his full bladder. The dirt roads, distance driving, and bottles of water made it hard to hold it in. He urinated on the side of the road, got back in his truck, and proceeded to continue to drive.

As he glanced out at the horizon in the open fields, he saw something. He couldn't make it out at first. The figure was black and odd-looking. He thought maybe it was a sick calf. He stopped, got out of the vehicle, and approached. As he walked closer, he realized it was not a calf at all. It was a badly burned naked woman in horrible shape. He paused, took a deep breath, and bowed his head as he continued on. Roylynn looked at Steve and uttered, "Water."

Steve was taken aback. He ran back to his truck to retrieve his sleeping bag. He searched for water, but he'd drank all that. All he had left was a can of warm Diet Coke. He grabbed the sleeping bag and the Diet Coke. He walked back to her and wrapped the sleeping bag around her. He put the bottle of Diet Coke in her badly burned mouth. Her lips were missing, so he lifted the Diet Coke to her mouth. It just ran down her face and chest.

He set it down, went back to the truck, and found the straw that he tried to throw out in the back of the pick-up. He picked it up, looked up to the sky, and said, "thank you, God." He walked back to Roylynn, put the straw in the bottle, and put it back up to her mouth. She grabbed the straw with her teeth and began to drink.

He let her drink for a bit and then scooped her up in his arms. He carried her back to his truck. He gently placed her in the passenger seat and drove towards the Crow hospital. He kept his eyes on the road. He tried not to stare at her too much. He kept praying to himself. He hoped that they made it to the hospital on time.

Roylynn sat in the passenger side and just stared out the window. She looked at Steve for a long time and silently thanked God for sending her an angel. They remained silent as they each were lamenting on her rescue. On his way to town, he was able to flag down a BIA officer.

"Oh my God!" the BIA officer said, "what the hell?" He could not believe his eyes. He'd never seen anything like this before.

"You've got to help me," Steve replied. "I found her out in my field. My God, I thought she was a dead cow. It's unbelievable."

"Did you get a name or anything?"

"Yeah, she said her name is Roylynn Rides Horse, and she knows who did this to her. We've got to get her to the hospital now."

"I'll radio ahead; I think I have some more blankets in my vehicle. I'll go get them and radio this in. Then you can follow me in."

The officer walked back to his vehicle and grabbed some blankets. He picked up his radio and buzzed the Crow Agency hospital.

"Hey, I'm bringing a burn victim in. Female. Badly burned. You're probably going to want to call a Salt Lake chopper. You'll need to stabilize her until they show up. We'll be there shortly."

The officer walked back to Steve's vehicle. He covered her with blankets he had in his vehicle. He tried to communicate with Roylynn.

"Here you go, ma'am," he said as he wrapped the blankets around her. "This should help some. We're gonna get you taken care of. Just hang in there. OK"

Roylynn nodded.

"Do you know who did this to you?" he asked.

Roylynn nodded.

"Ok, well, we'll get that information at the hospital. Just hang in there."

The officer ran back to his vehicle, got in, and turned on his lights and sirens. He sped away with Steve right behind him. They made their way to the hospital, where she named her assaulters. Once stabilized, she was life-flighted to the burn trauma intensive care unit at the University of Utah Healthcare hospital in Salt Lake City, UT.

Roylynn was found by Steve Peterson fourteen hours after her brutal attack. She was badly beaten. She suffered burns over 45% of her body. She underwent over thirty surgeries. Both of her feet were amputated due to severe frostbite. She endured numerous skin grafts. 90% of her skin grafts came from the healthy skin on her back that was not affected when she was set on fire. The fire stripped her of a breast, her lips, and her eyelids. Her family never left her side. She survived for 67 days.

She was able to name every single one of her assaulters. One of her male assaulters was arrested at his home. His girlfriend, who he was with at the time of his arrest, was wearing Roylynn's clothes. The assailants were all tried and convicted by a grand jury. They were sentenced to prison and are currently serving time for their heinous crimes.

Roylynn's family continues to tell her story and keep her in the spotlight so she is not forgotten. They pray daily to cope with the loss of their beautiful Lynnie Girl.

Bonnie Three Irons

Say Her Name

May 31, 1982 – April 10, 2017

For God so loved the world that he gave his one and only Son, that whoever believes in him shall not perish but have eternal life. John 3:16

⁚⁚

Jennifer White Bear clocked out of work at six o'clock pm. She said good bye to a fellow co-worker and headed home. Her daughter Bonnie, who worked at a local bakery, invited her auntie over. She planned on cooking a big meal for everyone, as she had the next day off.

It was Friday evening and Bonnie was excited to be spending that time with family. She loved to cook for everyone and she did it as often as she could. Bonnie's meals were amazing. She was a great cook. She always went above and beyond by showing her love for everyone in her cooking.

Bonnie was working her magic in the kitchen that night. She had a feast big enough to feed an army cooking, when Jennifer walked in the house.

"Oh, my Bonnie, it smells so good. You are outdoing yourself again, aren't you? "Jennifer said as the aroma coming from the kitchen over took her senses.

"It's my specialty mom." Bonnie replied as she tended to the hot stove top and oven. "We'll be eating like queens."

"You amaze me." Jennifer told her daughter. "You simply amaze me. You really should own your own restaurant."

"Ah mom, I love the bakery. Getting everyone fattened up with my delicious cakes, donuts, and pastries." Bonnie replied with a smile.

"It's no lie you make the best cakes. Did you bring one home with you?"

"Aye, you know I did. I wouldn't leave my home girls without desert."

"So, who all is coming over?"

"Just Auntie Sister, and you of course, and the kids." Bonnie replied as she grabbed a stack of plates from the cupboard. "Since you are here, will you help set the table?"

"Of course, I will." Jennifer took the plates from Bonnie's arms and began to set the table. She was looking forward to seeing Jayla. It made her heart happy that Bonnie and Jayla still hung out and remained friends after high school. Jayla was more than just an auntie. She was more like a sister. Jennifer watched the two girls grow up together. They form such a close bond.

Jayla walked through the door. "Hello, the queen has arrived!" She exclaimed as she entered the house. She took off her jacket, and gave Bonnie a hug.

"Hello Cousin," Jayla said as she gave Jennifer a hug. "It's so good to see you. Oh my does it smell good in here!"

"Yeah, have a seat. Dinner is almost done. It's a good thing I told you to be here at six o'clock." She as she looked at her watch. The time read 6:45.

"Ah, Crow time. Good thinking auntie." Jayla replied as she poured herself a glass of ice water.

"Kids! Dinner's ready!!" Bonnie shouted as she placed the cooked food into serving dishes and placed it in the center of the table. The kids came running to the table, eager to be the first to serve themselves a good-sized helping of every delectable dish Bonnie had just served.

"Hey now, did you all wash your hands before you came running in here?" Bonnie asked her kids.

They all nodded their heads, and held up their hands to show her they were clean. "I don't think you had enough time to wash them. Go back and do it again. Only clean hands at my table."

The kids scampered off, quickly washed and dried their hands. Then they rushed back to the dinner table.

"Let me see." Bonnie said. The kids showed their clean hands to their mother and flashed gleaming smiles for her approval so they could be seated and enjoy her good cooking. They joined her, Jennifer, and Jayla at the table. Bonnie was extremely happy to put food on the table for her family.

"Oh Bonnie, you've outdone yourself once again. I'm so stuffed." Jennifer said as she got up from the table and started to clear the empty dishes.

"Aye, you finished first and touched the first empty plate! That means you're doing all the dishes." Jayla said as she pushed herself away from the table. She headed towards the basement. "I'll go start up the Play Station." The kids followed her.

"Don't you want dessert?!" Bonnie yelled down the stairs.

"Dessert!?" they yelled, as they scampered back up the stairs. "Of course, we want dessert!"

"I always have room for dessert" said one of the children.

"As long as chocolate is involved, then count me in!" Jayla grinned.

Bonnie set the cake on the table. She served everyone a nice sized slice. Everyone smiled. Bonnie's cakes were the best and they were in for a real treat.

After they ate their large slices of cake they headed back downstairs. Bonnie helped her mom clean up the kitchen.

"Go join Jayla and the kids" Jennifer said, "I'll clean up the kitchen for you. You did such a fantastic job, don't worry about this mess. I've got this."

Bonnie headed out of the kitchen and headed downstairs to the "girl cave" to join Jayla and her kids and play video games. Usually, the kids took over the controls. Bonnie ended up just watching them have fun together. She loved to see her children all together laughing and having fun together. Soon it was bedtime for the kids.

"Come on kids, it's time for bed. Upstairs you go. Make sure to give grandma lots of kisses before you hop in bed" Bonnie said to the kids.

"Awe, mom, do we have to go to bed so soon?" they chimed, "Can't we just have five more minutes?"

"Yes, you have to. Just like every other night." Bonnie chuckled to herself. The kids always tried to extend staying up by just five more minutes. She followed the kids upstairs to tuck them into bed and say goodnight. Then she went back down stairs to join Jayla.

"Hey, let's go out." Jayla said to Bonnie

"Why you wanna do that? We are fine here." Bonnie replied.

"Ah come on auntie, let's go have some fun. I'll call the gang and we'll go have some real fun." Jayla said. "Why do you want to stay home? You're acting like an old woman. Don't you have tomorrow off?"

"Ok, if you insist." Bonnie replied. The two ladies got up and went upstairs and grabbed their jackets. It was a chilly April evening. Spring was arriving and the air was still cool and crisp.

"Mom!" Bonnie yelled to Jennifer. "Mom, you up?"

"Shhhh… the kids are almost asleep." Jennifer scolded.

Bonnie smiled. "Mom, we're gonna go out for a while. We're going to go meet up with our friends".

"Don't stay out too late. Remember I work tomorrow."

"Ok, I won't. I love you mom. See you in the morning." Bonnie said as she put her two hands together and formed a heart with her fingers. She placed it over her heart and moved it back and forth. She turned around and walked out the door.

The next morning Jennifer got up early. The house was quiet and still. Everyone was still sleeping. She went to the kitchen, put on a pot of coffee, and looked out the window. She quietly crept down the stairs to see if Bonnie was sleeping. She went downstairs and looked around. No one was there.

She continued to get ready for work. When it was almost time for her to leave, she knocked on Bonnie's bedroom door. "Bonnie, you in there?" Jennifer asked quietly as she slowly opened the door. Bonnie's bed was empty.

"Hmm… where could she be?" Jennifer thought. "That little shit was supposed to be home." She muttered to herself. She was annoyed that Bonnie didn't return home like she said she would the night before.

Jennifer then called Bonnie but there was no answer. Then she tried Jayla, but she didn't answer her phone either. She tried to call one of Bonnie's other closest friends. Again, no one answered.

Jennifer woke up one of the teenagers. "Hey, grandma's gotta go into work. Your mom isn't home yet. I'm sure she'll be here soon. Keep an eye on the littles OK."

"Ok" the teenager said. She rubbed her eyes, yawned, and fell back asleep.

Jennifer went to work. She had a feeling in the pit of her stomach that something wasn't right. It wasn't like Bonnie to not come home at all. She hadn't called, left a message, or anything. That was out of character for Bonnie. Jennifer couldn't quite put her finger on it, but she knew something was very wrong.

That day was per cap day. Bonnie's license plates were due to be paid. Jennifer knew Bonnie had the day off and would be taking care of her affairs. She tried calling her daughter all that day, but she never answered. Jennifer grew concerned. When her shift was over, she clocked out and went home.

"Bonnie!" She shouted. "You home!?" There was no answer.

Jennifer called Bonnie's oldest teenager. "Hey there, it's grandma. Did your mom show up?"

"Nah, she never did. So, we came over here to dad's house. Tell her we're over here okay." The teenager replied.

"Ok. I will when I see her. Tell your dad to call me when he can."

"Ok, will do. Love you grandma."

"Love you too dear. Talk to you later."

Jennifer hung up. "Where is that girl?" she muttered. Jennifer looked around the house. There was no sign that Bonnie had been home at all. She tried calling Jayla. Again, there was no answer. "Well, she'll show up eventually." She said to herself as she settled in for the night to wait for Bonnie to return.

Jennifer sat on the living room couch and watched TV to help the time go by as she waited for Bonnie to come home. The hours passed, and there was still no sign of Bonnie. Finally, around midnight, Jennifer couldn't keep her eyes open any longer. She fell asleep.

The next morning, Jennifer woke up on the couch in the clothes she'd changed into when she got off work the day before. She went into the kitchen, made a pot of coffee, and looked out the kitchen window. Bonnie's car was still sitting there with the expired plate still unchanged. Jennifer looked around the house. There was still no sign of her.

Jennifer grabbed her cell phone and dialed Jayla again. Still no answer. She dialed one of the friends that she figured had been out with Jayla and Bonnie two nights ago.

"Hello!"

"Yeah, hey, is Bonnie with you? I haven't seen or heard from her for two days now. Have you seen her? Do you know what's going on?" Jennifer said frantically.

"Hold up, calm down. Yeah, she's with Jayla."

"Well, I've tried to call her several times, and she isn't answering."

"I dunno, maybe she lost her phone."

"Both of them? "

"Hey, I dunno. All I know is she isn't with me. If she ain't with Jayla, then I don't know where she is."

"Okay, thanks," Jennifer said as she hung up. She did not have a good feeling at all about any of this. This wasn't like Bonnie not to call or show up. It was strange that her cousin was blowing her off and not taking her calls.

Jennifer called her grandchildren's father. "Hey, is Bonnie with you?"

"Nah, she hasn't come here. She's pissing me off, to be honest. She hasn't called or anything. Today is our little girl's birthday. Maybe she'll meet up with us at Chuckie Cheese. She wouldn't miss her baby girl's birthday. See you there in a couple of hours."

"Yeah, see you in a couple of hours," Jennifer replied. She hung up the phone. She was racking her brain, wondering why Bonnie wasn't home. Why hadn't she called? Why hadn't she touched base with her kids or anything? This was so out of character for her. It wasn't like her at all. Jennifer got ready for her granddaughter's birthday. She got in her car and drove to Billings to meet Bonnie and the kids for the birthday party.

Jennifer arrived at Chuckie Cheese. She walked in the entrance with gifts in hand for her granddaughter. She located her grandkids and ex-son-in-law. Bonnie was not there. "Where's Bonnie?" She asked.

"I don't know, she hasn't come yet. Maybe she's running on Crow Time."

Jennifer gave a nervous smile. "Yeah, that must be it." She replied.

The party got underway. Halfway through pizza and large animated stuffed characters singing and dancing, there was still no sign of Bonnie. Jennifer was texting her and calling her. There was no response. Before she knew it, the party ended. The kids were exhausted, and Bonnie had still not shown up.

By the time Jennifer got home, it was very late. She was exhausted, and she had to work the next day. She decided that if Bonnie wasn't home when she got home from work, she would go out and start looking for her on her own. Jennifer told herself that Bonnie would show up the next day and that there would be a damn good explanation for all of this.

Jennifer got home from work the next day, and still, there was no sign of Bonnie. Jennifer got in her car and started driving. She was going to find her daughter. She called Jayla, and she finally answered.

"Where have you been? Where's Bonnie?" She demanded.

"I don't know she didn't leave with me?" Jayla replied.

"What do you mean she didn't leave with you? Your friend told me she did."

"No, she left with somebody else."

"You are lying!" Jennifer cried.

"No, I'm not. I swear she didn't leave with me. I saw her leave with someone else. They were going to go drinking and then go home."

"Why haven't you been answering my calls?"

"Because I had to wait to get my per cap so I could pay for the bill this next month. I was out of minutes."

"Oh, okay, well, why isn't Bonnie answering?"

"How would I know? Maybe the same reason."

Jennifer hung up the phone in frustration. She was getting nowhere with Jayla or any of Bonnie's other friends. No one seemed to know or was concerned that Bonnie was nowhere to be found. She continued to drive around. She stopped at a few houses of some people who knew Bonnie. She asked if they'd seen her. Everyone just shook their heads no. Jennifer was left with so many questions and absolutely no answers.

Jennifer continued on. She took some back roads and searched all the local hang-out spots. There was no sign of Bonnie. Everyone she asked or showed Bonnie's picture to had not seen her. No one gave Jennifer any clues or insight that would lead her to her daughter.

Jennifer spoke to many of Bonnie's friends. They either didn't answer their phone or their door. The ones who did all said they saw Bonnie leave with someone else. None of their stories added up. She was frustrated that some people she was trying to reach were outright avoiding her.

The next day, Jennifer decided it was time to file a missing person's report with the Crow police. She was afraid that too many days had passed with no word from Bonnie. She was kicking herself for not doing this sooner. She knew if she had, she would have gotten nowhere. The cops would have just told her to wait a few days.

She waited a few days. She searched on her own and to no prevail. Jayla was supposed to meet her at the police station, but she was a no-show. Jennifer couldn't understand why Jayla had suddenly become so flakey and acting so strange. Deep down, she was starting to wonder if she knew something or perhaps was feeling guilty.

The police told Jennifer to give it a few more days. They told her that Bonnie would eventually show up. Jennifer explained to them that she'd already given it a few days. She begged for their help. They handed her a stack of paperwork to fill out and told her to come back in a few days if she didn't turn up. She grabbed the paperwork and left.

She had a feeling that Bonnie was already gone. Rumors were swirling that that the last time anyone saw Bonnie, she was in the Wolf Mountains. It was reported that she had gotten into a fight with someone and then walked off. No one said exactly who she was fighting with or what they had been fighting about.

There was no cell phone service that far out of town in the mountains. Bonnie wouldn't have been able to call anyone for help. It was much too far for someone to walk home on a cold April night in the mountains.

Frustrated, Jennifer contacted a man from the nearby town of Pryor and asked if he could put together a search party. This is what he did, and he was good at it. Cary Lance, with the aid of Jennifer and others from the community that he had called upon, formed a search party.

They began the search where she was last seen, the sight where they'd heard a fight had taken place. They located her footprints on a gravel dirt road and followed them. Only one set of footprints was located, indicating that she was walking alone.

Her footprints followed the dirt road. Twice, they left the road and went into some timber. It appeared as if she had stopped there to hide. Then her footprints went back to the dirt road.

The search team followed Bonnie's footprints for 6.3 miles from where the alleged fight took place. Suddenly, the footprints stopped abruptly. They just ended. They didn't pick up anywhere else at all.

The search team spread out from out where her footprints ended. Two hundred yards away, one of the searchers found Bonnie. It seemed like Bonnie had just floated away from the spot on the road to where she was found in some brush.

She was lying on the ground with her head facing downhill. Her arms and legs were outstretched. Her jacket was pulled up above her waistline. She was missing one shoe. By the time she was found, her body was bloated and had a purplish discoloration to it. The Big Horn County Coroner was called. He came and recovered her remains. He determined her cause of death to be hypothermia.

After Bonnie's lifeless body was discovered and the coroner had meticulously prepared her for her final rest, an unexpected and perplexing occurrence transpired. Jennifer, overcome with grief, arrived with a set of garments meant to clothe Bonnie in preparation for her funeral. However, when she inquired about the clothing Bonnie had been wearing when she was found, the coroner delivered an astonishing revelation: those very garments had been incinerated. Despite Jennifer's growing unease, the coroner remained steadfast in his assurance that no sinister events were at play.

To this day, no one has come forward to divulge exactly what had happened the night Bonnie left her home for a night out with friends. Friends that she considered family and knew most of her life.

Two women who were with Bonnie that night have since passed away. One woman suspected to have fought with Bonnie the night she disappeared died in an alcohol-related single-vehicle car accident not long after Bonnie's body was found. Another woman last seen with Bonnie died from alcoholism.

Jennifer, Bonnie's mother, is still left without answers or justice for her daughter's death. She continues to pray each day that someday, someone will come forward with the truth.

Baby It's Cold Outside

∴

The Sovereign Bodies Institute lists six cases of hypothermia as a cause of death in Montana in their database of missing and murdered. Four of those cases are from Big Horn County. Three of those four occurred in the last three years.

Hypothermia is something we tend to think of when someone falls through the ice into the water in the winter. According to articles in the International Journal of Legal Medicine, those most at risk for hypothermia include senior citizens, the mentally ill, the homeless, and those addicted to drugs and alcohol. Men and women aged 65 and older are most susceptible to hypothermia, and men are more prone to suffer from hypothermia than women.

Yet data gathered by The Sovereign Bodies Institute reveal four cases of hypothermia in Big Horn County happened to young women. A 14-year-old, a 16-year-old, a 17-year-old, and a 35-year-old. These four young women didn't fall through the ice into frigid waters. They certainly don't fit the generic risk group for hypothermia, yet all of their deaths were ruled as accidental hypothermia.

Scientifically, hypothermia occurs when the core body temperature drops below 95 degrees. It is classified into three categories or stages: mild, moderate, and severe.

Mild hypothermia is described as experiencing shivering, weakness, drowsiness, and confusion. In the mild stage, a person will still have some logical thinking skills and may try to do things to stay warm, such as move around.

As the body's core temperature decreases, the person shifts to moderate hypothermia, where the skin can become pale. The blood in the body from the outer extremities rushes to the heart in order for the heart to pump blood to the vital organs to try to keep the body warm. This places great stress on the heart. It can cause the heart to beat irregularly. Shivering increases as the body tries to stay warm. With prolonged shivering, the muscle groups in the lower extremities become exhausted, and blood begins to return to the freezing extremities.

The hypothermic victim will perceive this as extreme warmth and will begin to undress. This phenomenon of undressing when freezing to death is called "paradoxical undressing." It is an extremely common behavior for people dying of hypothermia because they actually feel very hot.

Another self-protective primitive measure taken at this stage if the core body temperature drops slowly is "terminal burrowing" or "hide–and–die syndrome." The person will act like a hibernating animal in a last-ditch effort to remain warm. The brain temperature and function will then decrease, resulting in a person suffering from amnesia, slurred speech, and cognitive decline. Physical coordination becomes difficult in this stage.

When the body's core temperature reaches 78.8 degrees, the body is now experiencing severe hypothermia. At this stage, major organs become too cold and too weak to function properly. The pulse becomes extremely slow. The person will slip into a comatose state. Electrolyte imbalances in the bloodstream take place, followed by complete organ failure. The heart stops as a result of prolonged exposure to the cold. Death at this point is inevitable.

Exposure to water, high winds, wind chill, excessive sweating, underlying medical conditions, certain medications, age, and alcohol intake can all speed up the hypothermic response. Most of the hypothermic deaths occur in the winter months between December and February.

The identification of hypothermia as the primary cause of death has always been somewhat problematic in forensic pathology. This is due to unspecific, inconstant, or even negative macroscopic and microscopic findings, according to the International Journal of Legal Medicine.

When coroners, pathologists, medical examiners, and doctors fill out death certificates, it is usually based on their best guestimate as to the cause of death. Death certificates are the basic source of information on mortality. The cause of death listed is entered into a vital data bank. It is then used for statistical analysis, according to Dr. Annie Bukacek.

Dr. Bukacek states that causes of death listed on the death certificate are normally based on educated guesses and assumptions that go unquestioned. A death certificate has a 60% chance of being more accurate if that person dies in the hospital or has some kind of terminal condition. Suppose a person dies before labs, x-rays, or physical exams can evaluate them. In that case, there can be unclear possibilities for their death, especially if they did not die from something that leaves nothing to the imagination, such as a gunshot wound or physical bodily trauma.

Autopsies are not always performed unless foul play is suspected or the person is a ward of the state. The point being is that not every single person who dies has an autopsy. For example, if a person dies at home, a family member can vouch for the reason of death to the funeral home, and that cause of death will be listed even though someone with no medical degree gave it.

The International Journal of Legal Medicine further indicates death by hypothermia is very difficult to verify because there are no diagnostic autopsy findings. Some things can be suggestive and can be diagnosed solely on circumstantial evidence. As a consequence, death by hypothermia is made by a combination of observations. It includes an appropriate history of exposure, certain nonspecific pathological findings such as frostbite, and an array of other things if present. It also takes into account the absence of other obvious lethal factors.

With all of this information laid out, it's easy to see why the families of the young ladies whose deaths were ruled as hypothermia are demanding better answers for their untimely, unnecessary deaths. Young, healthy, athletic women don't just randomly wander away from friends and known areas of shelter into vastly wide-open fields and die from hypothermia.

Henny Leslie Scott

Neso'eoo'e (Twenty Stands Woman)

Say Her Name

January 9, 2004 – December 8, 2018

Walk as tall as the trees, Live strong as the mountains, be as gentle as the spring winds, keep the warmth of the summer sun in your heart, and the Great Spirit will always be with you.

~Native American Proverb~

❋

Henny Scott was a vibrant fourteen-year-old girl from Lame Deer, MT. She was full of hope and aspiration, like many girls her age. She was well-liked by everyone who knew her and came into contact with her. She was very outgoing and was everyone's friend.

Her mom says she always gave her all and did her best in everything. She lit up every room she walked in. Her passions were track, basketball, hunting, and art. She was an A honor roll student. She dreamed of becoming a doctor when she grew up. She was often times caught studying her mom's EMT books. She was a very good artist. For a short time, some of her art was featured in an art gallery in Billings, MT.

As the new high school year had started, Henny was making new friends. She was coming of age, and the cute boys at school noticed who she was. She was changing from a little girl in middle school to a blossoming woman in high school. The new school year began with her impressing new friends.

A very cute boy asked her out. The two of them had started to hang out a little more and get to know each other. She was really starting to like him.

One day, she invited him and a couple of her friends over to her house. They were hanging out, sitting on the front porch, laughing and giggling. Henny was coy and nervously tossing her hair from shoulder to shoulder as she subtly threw hints that she was interested in this boy.

"You're a slut!" He said from out of nowhere.

Her friend immediately came to her side.

"I'll punch you in the face next time you disrespect my girl like that, you little punk." Her friend said."

"Eh, no worries. I'm just joshing around," he said.

Henny scowled, "I think you need to leave."

He shook his head, got up, and walked away.

"You ok?" Her friend asked.

"Yeah, I'm fine," Henny said as she entered the house. She was disgusted that the boy she really liked turned out to be such a jerk.

She stormed past her mom, Paula, on her way to her bedroom to cry alone.

"Henny…" Paula said when Henny passed her. She kept walking, trying to conceal her tears.

Paula looked at Henny's friend standing on the porch. Her friend shrugged her shoulders.

"He's a jerk." She said as she turned around and left to go home.

Paula knocked on Henny's door, "Henny, you OK?"

"Go away," She sobbed.

"Maybe I can help," Paula replied.

She knew all too well what a broken heart felt like. She had been a teen once upon a time ago. "You know I was fourteen once, too."

"I'm fine. He's nothing but a jerk. I'm so stupid to like him."

"No, you aren't Henny. He's stupid to be a jerk. If he's a jerk, you are better off not liking him."

Henny slowly opened the door a crack and looked at her mom with tears in her eyes.

"Come here," Paula said as she reached her arms out to give her a hug.

"It'll be OK. You are beautiful. You just be you and keep your nose in the books instead of on the boys." Paula tried comforting her, and Henny cracked a smile.

"Thanks, Mom," She answered.

That school year was full of ups and downs for Henny. She was a busy teen getting pulled in different directions. The A student, the athlete, the artist, keeping up with her old friends and trying to impress upon new ones. She was busy being a good role model for her younger siblings. She was busy trying to be a good daughter. But she was also trying to assert her independence and getting grounded for the times she overstepped her boundaries.

Things would be going great for a while, but then they wouldn't. One day, her friends told her they were best friends for life. Then, the next day, they'd show up at her house, threatening to beat her up because of their teenage insecurities and jealousy. It's the life of most freshman girls.

It was a day like most other days. Henny did her usual morning routine and went to school. That Friday was an early release day. She came home, dropped off all her school work that was due on Monday, and changed her clothes.

"Hey, Mom, can I go to the open gym?" She asked.

"Well…" Paula drifted.

"Please, Mom!?" Henny pleaded. She put her hands together and gave her best teenage smile that no parent could say no to.

"Ok, fine, you can go, but you must be home before your dad gets home from work. You are supposed to be grounded; you know."

"Thank you, Mom, you are the best! I promise I will," Henny replied, "I'll even do extra chores tomorrow; I swear."

An hour later, a black truck honked at the house. Henny jumped up off the couch. "Bye, Mom! Love you!" Henny yelled as she picked up her jacket and purse and walked out the front door. She raised her arm up in the air and waved good bye to her mother.

"Love you too! Don't forget to be home on time!" Paula shouted back as she watched her daughter walk away without realizing that would be the last time she would see her.

Right before it was time for Henny to be home, Paula's phone rang. It was Henny. "Hey, Mom, I'm having such a great time with my friends. Is it OK if I go to the Native American Classic Basketball games with them?" She asked.

"No, Henny, I don't want you going to Billings. You are still grounded, remember?" Paul replied. "It's time for you to come home. Are you still at school? I'll come and pick you up if you need me to."

"No, I'm at the twin's mom's house. I'll get a ride from them. I'll be home in a bit."

"Ok, is their mom home? It sounds like there's a few people there." Paula inquired.

"Nah, she's not here; it's just the twins and a couple more friends."

"Ok, see you soon. Love you."

"Love you too, Mom," Henny said with a discouraged voice. She was so disappointed she couldn't go to the games with her friends. The Native American Classic was a big deal; she hated missing it. She hung up her phone.

"So, did your mom say yes?" One of the twins asked.

"No. She said no. I have to go home. Can you give me a ride?"

"Nah, you have to wait."

"Wait, wait for what?"

"I dunno; wait for someone to give you a ride home."

Henny waited patiently. Before she knew it, she found herself stuck with some so-called friends who decided to turn the evening into a small house party. She was at a house six miles from town with people that she was just getting to know. Someone brought alcohol, and before she knew what was happening, she gave into peer pressure to take a sip of alcohol.

One sip turned into two. Disgusted with the taste of it, she wanted to leave. This was not what she had planned for the evening.

"Eh, you want another one?" someone asked as they cracked open a new beer for her.

"No," Henny replied as she pushed it away from her. "I need to go home."

She stood up but suddenly experienced being tipsy for the first time. She knew she had to get home. No one was in any shape to give her a ride.

It was getting late. Henny was annoyed no one could give her a ride home. She was afraid to call her mom or step dad to come and pick her up. She'd be grounded for life if she did. Let alone she wouldn't be able to face the shame from her friends for acting like a prude. She decided to wait it out until the morning when someone was sober to give her a ride. It was too cold and far to walk. She decided to face the consequences of being grounded for life in the morning.

Paula paced the floor of her home, wondering why Henny was not home yet. Minutes turned into hours. There was no word or sight of Henny. Paula checked Henny's social media profiles. She also checked Henny's friend's profiles. Nothing, absolutely nothing. Paula knew something was wrong. She couldn't put her finger on it. She had a gut feeling that something was not right.

Suppose she had only been stern with her daughter and stood her ground on making her stay home. But Henny was such a good kid, pulling good grades and making curfew. Paula's mind went back and forth on whether she decided to let Henny go out before the time had lapsed on her grounding.

But there were only two days left to the grounding. She didn't think ending it early was a big deal, just giving her a curfew. She couldn't understand why all of her calls and texts were going unanswered. A very exhausted Paula finally went to bed. Her husband told her to get some rest and would stay up and wait for her to come home.

Paula's husband, Nate, woke her up the next morning and let her know Henny did not come home. It was time to trade shifts in waiting for her. She groggily unplugged her phone from the charger and checked it for messages. There were none.

She once again took to social media. There were no posts from Henny or any of her friends or photos. Paula thought that was very strange. Kids are constantly taking photos of themselves with their friends and posting them on several different social media outlets. It was great Paula could keep track of Henny so easily. Every parent of a teenager dreams about this. Your teenager says they are at a game, and you know for sure they are there because they are posting score updates and selfies with their friends, having a good time.

Paula poured herself a cup of coffee. She sat at the table and decided to take to social media to find her daughter. She started posting on Henny's friend's Facebook pages, "Hey, did you see Henny last night?" She didn't want her friends to know Henny was in deep serious trouble, so she tried to keep things light in order to get a response.

She only received a few responses: "No, I didn't see her last night" or "she wasn't with us." Paula wished she had known who was driving the black truck that Henny had left in. She'd never seen that person before.

"Why didn't I know something was off right then and there?" She asked herself.

Paula spent most of the day scouring social media and trying to act bravest for her other kids. She felt bad that she was lying to them through her teeth, pretending everything was alright. The big sister they looked up too was nowhere to be found. Paula did not want the other kids to worry. She would do all the worrying. That was her job as a mom.

The day after Henny didn't return home, it came and went. There was no sign or word from her. A weary Paula decided to call it a night. She would devise a plan the next day if Henny hadn't returned. Again, her husband took the night shift. He waited all night for Henny so Paula could regroup the next day. The hours on the clock ticked away as Nate waited for his daughter to walk through the front door. He stood and jumped up at the sound of every noise he heard, thinking it was her. Every car that passed by grabbed his attention, hoping they would slow down and pull into the driveway. Not one single one of them did; they just kept a steady pace and drove on by.

Paula awoke the next morning. She opened the door to Henny's room and saw an empty bed. She walked through the living room by her husband, who was asleep, propped upright on the couch with his mouth gaping open. She went to the kitchen and made a pot of coffee. She added an extra scoop of coffee grounds. They were both going to need coffee first. She walked over and gently nudged her husband awake. He slowly came, and the first words out of his mouth were, "Is Henny home?" Paula shook her head.

Nate finished his coffee, went to his room, and changed into a fresh set of clothes. He grabbed his car keys and drove to the twin's house. Instinct and intuition told him to start here. When Henny last spoke with his wife, she had mentioned the twins. The house was not too far from town, so he figured it wouldn't take long and was hoping that Henny would be there. He was remaining hopeful that he would return home with his daughter.

Nate pulled into the driveway. The house looked quiet. He parked the car, exited, and walked up to the front door. He knocked but there was no answer. He knocked again, only harder. A minute later, a woman answered the door.

"Can I help you?" She said.

"Yeah, I'm looking for my daughter Henny. Is she here?" Nate asked.

"Nah, there's nobody here but me." She replied.

Nate tried to look inside. The woman opened the door wide enough so he could see there was no one else in her house. He turned away and walked back to his car, feeling defeated. He really hoped he would find her there.

Paula was spending her day making a missing person's flier and posting it to every garage sale site she could find in the area. She wasn't getting anywhere with Henny's friends, so she figured, why not reach out to the community? She even posted on the larger city of Billings garage sale sites. Henny mentioned she wanted to go there the night they last spoke. Maybe she went anyway and was still there.

Later that day, Paula received word of some sightings of her daughter. She was excited that someone saw her. One person posted a reply that they saw her in Busby. One person posted they saw a girl who looked like the girl on the flier in Lodge Grass. Another person said they saw a girl fitting that description in Crow.

When Paula probed the people responding, they gave a general area of the siting. Nate and Paula got in their car and started driving around the towns in the county, looking for Henny.

They were optimistic about the sightings. They drove and drove and drove. They held up Henny fliers asking people out and about if they'd seen their daughter. Everyone shook their heads. After hours of exhausting searching and dead ends, a defeated Nate and Paula headed home once again without their daughter.

The next day, Paula awoke, went through her new morning routine of checking her daughter's empty room, waking her husband up from the couch, making a strong pot of coffee, and scouring social media for new leads. This day was the day she would drive to the police station and file a missing person's report.

She arrived at the police station and asked to meet with an officer to file a missing person's report. An officer met her in the lobby of the station and started asking her questions. What was she wearing? When did you last see her? Who was she with? When did you last speak with her? Has she ever run away before? The last question, Paula hesitated. She started to answer yes but changed her answer to no.

"So, is it yes, or no?" The officer asked.

"It's complicated," She replied.

"Go on," The officer said.

"Well, she technically didn't run away. She got mad because her dad and I grounded her, so she thought she'd show us a thing or two by packing an overnight bag and staying with a friend for a weekend. It was her way of trying to tell us we can't tell her what to do because she's grown and all." Paula commented.

"So, she has run away before. Maybe she's at a friend's house asserting her grown up fourteen-year-old self," he said.

"No, this is different," Paula insisted.

"Before, she wasn't just gone. We knew exactly where she was. We knew exactly who she was with. She used their phones and posted all over social media. The other times, she answered my texts. This time, she isn't doing any of that," Paula demanded.

"She'll probably turn up sooner or later," The officer said as he closed his folder and stopped taking notes.

Paula looked at him in disbelief. She couldn't believe he was dismissing Henny as a spoiled runaway teen who didn't get her way after everything she told him. It wasn't like that at all. She was frustrated she got nowhere and went home feeling defeated yet again.

The next day, Paula and Nate took to social media again. Nate waited until the evening to pay a visit to the house where they suspected Henny was at last. He knew the mom worked the evening shift, so he hoped to talk to one of the kids when she wasn't around. Maybe one of them would know something.

That evening, Nate knocked on the door of the house where Henny had said she was a few nights ago. This time, a teenage boy answered the door after a few hard knocks.

"Hey, I'm Henny Scott's Dad," Nate said, "Is she here?"

"Nah, she ain't here," The boy said.

"Well, do you know where she might be?" Nate inquired.

"Nah," The teen replied.

"Ok, well, do you know where she might have gone? She was here a few nights ago, right." Nate pressed.

"Yeah, she was here. I dunno, she took off or something," He replied back.

"Took off…took off where?" Nate asked.

The teenage boy pointed towards a field, "I dunno, out that way, I guess."

"I guess?" Nate said quizzically.

"Yeah, I guess. I dunno," The teen responded.

"Can you be more specific?" Nate inquired, hoping for some answers.

"We had a party here a few nights ago. Henny was here. She got mad at me and took off into the field over there," He replied, pointing again to the field.

Nate looked to where the boy was pointing, noticing that the road was nearby to where he was pointing.

"So, where did she go after she got mad?" Nate further quizzed the teen.

"I dunno," He replied, "I tried to follow her, but it was cold, so I went back inside. Decided to just let her be. She was pretty mad."

"Hmmm… I see," Nate responded. "So, did she cool off and come back inside."

"Yeah, I dunno. Maybe, maybe not."

"Well, have you seen or heard from her since?"

"Nah, I guess she's pretty pissed, huh?"

"Yeah, she must be." Nate pondered.

There was a quiet moment where neither of them spoke. "Well, Ok then." The teen said as he shut the door, leaving Nate still standing there. He was trying to work the cryptic yet somewhat informative conversation through his mind. He turned around, surveyed the landscape and wondered why Henny would choose to run out into a field in the opposite direction of the road he had just driven in on. He walked back to his car. He was more confused than he was before he knocked on the door.

The next morning, Paula went through her routine again of checking for Henny in her room, waking up Nate in the living room, and making a strong pot of coffee. Each day, the coffee got a little bit stronger. Each day, Paula came up with new excuses to tell her other children as to why their big sister wasn't home yet again. Not knowing where her daughter was for so long now was painfully exhausting.

She had to stay strong. She couldn't let her mind wander. She hoped Henny would walk through the front door at any moment and everything would be alright. She just wanted her daughter home safe. She wanted to hold her daughter in her arms and hug her tight.

She placed a call to the police department, where she had first tried to file a missing person's report. She had new information. She called, and much to her dismay, they weren't interested in hearing the new information. They were still running with the assumption that she was just at a friend's house cooling off. They pretty much blew Paula off as a helicopter parent in denial that her daughter wasn't the sweet and innocent child they were convincing themselves she was.

Paula decided she would go to the neighboring town's police department and see if she could make headway with them. She decided she would file missing person's reports with every police department she could think of and then some. She would talk to every agency she could until she couldn't speak anymore.

She was getting new leads on social media. She would show those to the police until they listened and took her seriously. Henny wasn't some spoiled party girl who took off because she was mad about being grounded. Paula was perplexed as to why the authorities she spoke with made it seem that this was all that it was. Paula had a new feeling of hope, as this new department said they would open an investigation.

In the days that followed, an investigation was open. Nate and Paula found themselves amidst a swirl of police coming and going. They were answering questions and giving as much detail as possible. They remained optimist about finding their daughter once and for all. It wasn't long before the FBI was called in to assist.

Rumors began to circulate, and Nate and Paula found themselves attempting to sift through these rumors in order to ascertain what, if any, information they should place their trust in. One recurring theme that caught their attention was the claim that there had been a party at the house where Henny had claimed to be when she called her mother that night. Paula couldn't shake the feeling of how uncharacteristic this seemed for Henny.

She started to mentally beat herself up for not just driving over there after that call and picking her up herself. Once again, she went back and forth, playing out every scenario in her head, thinking of all the what-ifs. She blamed herself for letting her go that day. Nate could tell his wife was torturing and blaming herself for all of this. He didn't blame her. She was a good a good wife and a mother. Henny was a good kid. He hugged Paula and she broke down into a solid cathartic cry. This was the first time she really just let go of all her pent-up emotions. She'd remained so solid and strong up until this point. She was now suddenly letting go.

As the days passed, the investigation continued with no answers. Paula and Nate decided it was time to take matters into their own hands. The once hopeful investigation was becoming nothing but a disappointment. People weren't talking. The house Henny was last seen at wasn't taped off. It wasn't being treated as a crime scene. Nate and Paula had witnessed people coming and going as they pleased from that house.

"I'm so mad they can just walk in and out of there like nothing happened," Paula said to her husband.

"I agree, it's not right," He replied, "but what can we do?"

"Do you think it's time to reach out to White Buffalo and see if he can assemble a crew to help find her?" Paula asked.

Nate picked up his phone and dialed up White Buffalo.

"Hey Cary, it's me, Nate. We need your help."

"Sure man, what can I do for you?"

"Well, I'm sure you've heard Henny has been missing for a while now. I was wondering if you could assemble a team and help us. Paula and I are getting absolutely nowhere. We've been searching for answers on our own. The police, BIA, and FBI are all investigating, but you know how that is. Turning up a bunch of nothing. No one's talking to them."

"Yeah, sure, brother. I'll rally up my posse. Text me all the details."

"Thanks, man."

Nate turned to Paula. "He's on it."

Cary Lance made several phone calls. He asked everyone to meet at the community hall for a briefing using all the information Nate and Paula had texted him. The search party began their search for Henny's last known location. The house where a party had taken place. His team concentrated on searching near the house. They weren't allowed access inside the house. They weren't breaking any laws by walking around the grounds.

Later that day, a man who lived near the house told one of the searchers that he noticed some magpies swarming in the field about 200 yards from the house where Henny had been. He told them that the magpies usually eat his dog's food, but he noticed they were in a different area the last day or so. He pointed them out to a searcher.

The searcher located Cary to tell him this news. Cary launched a drone he had and began to do an aerial survey of the area. He concentrated on trying to determine what the magpies were paying attention to. He started to film when suddenly his drone went into its safety homing mode.

By the time he could move closer to the area where the magpies were, it was beginning to get dark, and the temperature was dropping. For the safety of his search team, he called them back to return to the community center. He would instruct them to assemble the next morning again at daybreak to continue the search and give them a new starting point. When Cary returned to the command center, his phone rang.

"Hello, this is White Buffalo," Cary answered.

"Yeah, this is Agent Smith. We found something, so there is no need for your team to return in the morning. We'll take it from here."

"10-4," Cary responded.

He told his team their work was done; they did not need to show up the next day.

The FBI took over from there. One of the agents pulled Paula and Nate aside.

"We've located your daughter," He stated.

"Can we see her? Where?" The questions blurted out of Paula's mouth.

"No, I'm sorry, not right now," He replied, "The best thing for you to do now is go home. We'll take it from here."

Nate and Paula were left without answers. They wanted to see their daughter.

The next day, Paula's phone rang.

"Hello," She answered.

"Yes, is this Paula Castro Stops?" The man on the other end said.

"Yes, who is this?" She inquired.

"I'm a reporter for the Billings Gazette. I'd like to give you my condolences on the death of your daughter. I'm so very sorry. I was wondering if I could get a word with you."

"The what? What did you just say?" Paula angrily asked.

"I'm sorry, did I catch you at a bad time?" He replied.

"What do you mean the death of my daughter? Who told you that preposterous information? She's not dead. We don't even know where she is." Paul snapped.

"I'm so sorry, Mrs. Stops. I'm sorry that this is the way you had to find out. I assumed you knew."

"Who told you this information?" She demanded.

"I received a press release from the Big Horn County Coroner about your daughter, Henny Scott. They found her deceased in a field out by the Muddy Creek area", He replied, "Look, I'm so sorry you are hearing this from me. This isn't the way it's supposed to happen. My God, I can't believe no one told you."

An infuriated Paula placed a call to the Big Horn County Coroner.

"Paula, so nice to speak with you," He said, "Will you be making funeral arrangements with me down at the mortuary."

"No, we won't. We want you to release her to the funeral home in Forsyth. I can't believe you didn't even have the decency to notify us."

"I'm sorry, it was out of my jurisdiction. I thought maybe someone else had told you."

"Well, I understand she was found in your county. Why wouldn't you think not to contact us? She's our daughter, for God's sake."

There was silence on the other end of the phone.

"Ok, I'll take her over to the Forsyth mortuary. You can see her there and work with them. I'll let them know you'll arrive tomorrow."

"Yes, please do. I want to see my daughter. I want to see for myself if it's actually her or not. No one has told us anything."

"Yes, OK. You'll be able to see her tomorrow."

The next day, Paula and Nate went to the mortuary in Forsyth, where their daughter's body was transferred per their request. They met with the funeral director. He had them pick out a casket.

"I'd like to go over your choices of caskets, and then I'll take you to see your daughter. Did you bring some clothes for us to dress her in for the funeral?"

"No, we'd like to see her first, then take her home and dress her. We'd like to have our traditional ceremony first."

"Ok, that is fine. The official cause of death determined by the medical examiner in Billings ruled her death as hypothermia. It shows there was no foul play. When you do see her, I hope you aren't expecting to find anything. We can't release her to you today; there are still some things we need to do. You can come back tomorrow. Please bring some clothes you want us to dress her in. Then we can prepare for you to collect her."

The next morning, they went to the funeral home to see their daughter and gave the mortician some clothes to dress her in so they could bring her home. This was the first time they were able to view her body. Paula saw her daughter for the first time since she left home almost two weeks ago.

Only now, she was lying on a cold metal gurney with a sheet covering her. The sheet was folded over so Paula and Nate could see her face. Paula gazed upon her face and confirmed this was indeed Henny. She stared at her beautiful daughter's lifeless body. Her vision blurred from the stream of tears that rolled down her cheeks. This was like a bad dream she had never envisioned in a million years. Nate handed the mortician the clothes. They arranged for them to pick Henny up the next day. Paula left the mortuary feeling completely numb.

The next day, Nate and Paula went to the funeral home to pick up their daughter and bring her home. They signed some papers, and the funeral home director handed over the clothes that she was wearing when she was brought in.

"Here, here are the clothes she was found in," he said as he handed them to Nate.

Paula grabbed the clear plastic bag and examined it. "Those are not the clothes Henny left my house in on that day. I've never seen these clothes before. These do not belong to Henny. Where are her clothes?" Paula questioned.

"I'm not sure. These were the clothes that were given to us by the coroner."

"There must be some kind of mix-up then," Paula replied.

"No, no mix-up, ma'am. These are hers," The mortician said.

Paula grabbed the bag of clothes and studied it intently. She'd never seen these clothes before. They left the funeral home with their daughter in the casket they picked out for her. They were going to take their baby girl home and have a traditional Cheyenne funeral. They hoped they could dress her in their traditional Cheyenne apparel, but there was no way that was possible now.

They moved her casket onto a wooden platform in a teepee that Nathan and some other relatives had prepared the day before just for Henny. This is where people would come to pay their respects before, they lay her to rest six feet below ground. Everything was perfect. Perfect as could be considering the circumstances.

Paula spent most of the first day in the teepee with Henny. She wasn't accepting the death certificate cause of death as hypothermia. It didn't make any sense. She was found only 200 yards from a house. How on earth could a fourteen-year-old girl that was surrounded by lots of people just run off into a field and die from hypothermia?

She began to examine her daughter's body lying in the casket. She stared at Henny's face and noticed something different. Her nose. Something wasn't quite right. A mother knows her child's face. Something was different about Henny's nose.

It looked like it may have been broken. Paula ran into the house and started scouring through her photos of her daughter. She looked through so many. She knew she wasn't losing her mind.

"Nate, you have to come with me to the teepee. Bring the camera." Paula said frantically.

"Ok, yeah, what's wrong?"

"Just come with me. Don't forget the camera."

Paula rushed out of the house to the teepee with the photo of Henny in her hand. Nate followed her with the camera in his hand. He was rushing out the door, still putting on his shoes.

"Look!" Paula exclaimed. "Look at my baby." She held up the photo next to Henny's face. "Do you see it? Tell me I'm not crazy."

Nate nodded. He looked at Paula as she looked back at him with a certain look in her eyes. She began to pull the clothes back Henny was wearing to expose as much bare skin as possible. She pointed out some scratches on Henny's arms, and Nate took photos. As Paula pulled back Henny's dress, she gasped. She discovered a cigarette burn mark on Henny's leg. Nate took more photos.

"Nate, what happened to our baby?" Paula cried. "She didn't die from hypothermia. That's total bullshit."

"What do we do?"

Paula shrugged. She didn't know the answer to that. She already knew that she didn't trust anyone who had been involved in the investigation or the people who handled her after she was found. Regardless, she was going to make some phone calls.

Paula called around to the investigators working on the case. She contacted the hospital that performed the autopsy and the coroner who had collected her body. None of them provided answers. They all told her the case was closed. Henny died from hypothermia, and that was it. They weren't going to further investigate.

They all told her there was no foul play involved. When Paula mentioned the broken nose, the scratches, and the cigarette burn, she was brushed off. They told her those things did not cause her death. They told her there could be all sorts of explanations for them. None of them would change their ruling of hypothermia.

Henny's visitation lasted for several days. Family and friends came to pay their respects. They brought Paula and Nate food for the family. A few of them made comments on Henny's misshapen nose. Paula was asked what she knew about that.

Paula listened closely to the teenagers that came to visit. She hoped to overhear something that would give her a clue about what happened, and overheard some gossip. She overheard a few things that explained the broken nose and scratches. The most disturbing thing she overheard during that time was that her daughter was assaulted and slammed on the floor at that party. Then, she was stuffed in a freezer. Her body was moved into the field when the heat and pressure of her search were turned up.

Their daughter was laid to rest. Things settled down. The visitation and funeral were over. Nate and Paula decided to inquire about getting a second opinion in another county. This was suggested to them by an outside investigator who caught wind of the story.

Two and a half years after Henny's burial, the family agreed to have Henny's body exhumed and re-examined by a renowned forensic pathologist. Unfortunately, by this time, too much time had passed. He was unable to determine a cause of death or shed any new light on unanswered questions. Nate and Paula seriously question who they can trust to handle it. With evidence most likely too old or destroyed and no one talking about the specifics of what happened that night, they have come up against a brick wall. They feel in their heart of hearts that their daughter did not die from hypothermia, but something much more sinister had happened on that fateful night.

I Want Your Sex

With the arrest, trial, and sentencing to 20 years in prison of Ghislaine Maxwell in 2022 and the arrest, suicide, and Netflix documentary on Jeffrey Epstein in 2019, sex trafficking has come front and center to the attention of everyone. Sex trafficking is certainly nothing new. It has been happening for centuries. Shockingly, it did not become illegal in the U.S. until the year 2000, when it was made a federal crime under the Trafficking Victims Protection Act.

According to the US Department of State, large events like the Super Bowl, the World Series, The NCAA college basketball tournaments, and political conventions are all havens for sex trafficking. Sex trafficking isn't just happening with influential elite people; it also occurs among gang members, migrant workers, prostitution rings, and the middle class. It involves businessmen, doctors, pharmacists, lawyers, federal agents, elected officials, coaches, and people you would least suspect. There are three tiers to trafficking: the seller, the buyer, and the victim.

According to Deliver Fund, the United States ranks as one of the worst countries in the world for human trafficking, with an estimated 199,000 incidents occurring annually. They cite that one in every five victims of human trafficking was believed to be children, exploited for child labor, child pornography, and begging. Trafficking takes place in large cities, small towns, and places in between. It can and does happen anywhere.

According to the Global Report on Trafficking in Person published by the United Nations, the most common form of human trafficking (79%) is sexual exploitation, of which 72% are girls. The second most common form of human trafficking

(18%) is forced labor, in which 66% are boys. Worldwide, almost 20% of all trafficking victims are children. The victims are predominately women and girls. The report also found that 30% of the countries reporting reported that women trafficking women was the norm.

Trafficking is covert, discreet, complex, and dynamic. It follows patterns, although every situation is unique. Victims of trafficking are mostly children, as children are easier to control. They are cheaper and are less likely to make demands. Children as young as six to nine years old are either kidnapped or groomed online into the dark underworld of sex trafficking. They are worth several thousand dollars per year to traffickers.

The National Foster Youth Institute cites that children raised in foster care stand a greater chance of being trafficked. In 2013, 60% of child victims recovered from sex trafficking by the FBI were from foster care. In 2017, 14% of missing children were being trafficked. A staggering 88% of those children had been in child welfare care.

Native American Indigenous girls are most particularly at risk. According to The Association of American Indian Affairs, 40% of all sex-trafficked women and girls in the US are Native American Indian.

According to the US Department of Homeland Security, trafficking isn't just about sex. Humans are trafficked for forced labor, marriage, and organ removal. Human trafficking globally brings in profits of roughly $150 billion a year for traffickers. The average age a girl enters into trafficking is 12-14 years old. The majority are runaways or victims of abuse.

Human trafficking can happen to anyone. However, some people are more vulnerable than others. People with special needs, mental health issues, substance abuse, homelessness, raised in foster care, and runaways are all vulnerable to traffickers. The trafficker uses their vulnerabilities to gain control and create dependency.

Traffickers use psychological means such as defrauding, manipulation, and threats in order to make their victims submissive to them. Teens with low self-esteem are manipulated into trafficking with lures of becoming a model. Traffickers set up fake modeling agencies. They dangle the proverbial carrot for young girls and boys, a chance to become something they never thought possible.

Her name was Anna, and she lived in the house whose backyard butted up to the backyard of the house I lived in. She wasn't the most attractive girl in the world. Her freckled face, strawberry blond hair, and crooked chicklet-sized teeth took away from any initial attraction she had. She was fit, though. The two of us would lay out and sun tan in our bikinis. The sun-kissed our toned, slender bodies. She said I looked exotic with my golden bronzed tan.

There was something a little deeper within Anna. I never really gave it much thought until recently. Behind her British accent, her hatred for American beer, the cute freckles, and strawberry blond hair, I believe Anna was involved in a sex trafficking ring of which I came close to being her prey.

It began with a phone call from a woman who was whispering. She identified herself as the woman who Anna worked for. The woman claimed she had been arrested for a DUI. She needed me to pick her up at her lawyer's office with one hundred dollars in cash to get her out of trouble. She told me that I had to keep this hush-hush. I wasn't to tell anyone. She didn't want her husband or any of the other neighbors to know she was in trouble.

I wasn't to tell a soul. I was to bring the cash, and one last thing, make sure to wear something nice but not stuffy. I hung up the phone with my mind spinning as to why the neighbor lady called me. I didn't even really know her.

I opened the patio door and stepped out onto the back deck. I tried to process the phone call I just received. I stared at her house and ran everything through my head. I looked up and saw a woman wearing a wide-brimmed straw hat, a short-sleeved blouse, and shorts. Her alabaster, somewhat cellulite-ridden legs gleamed brightly in the blazing summer sun.

My mouth dropped as this was the same figure I had seen several times from the patio deck. This was the same woman that Anna worked for. This was the same woman who was supposedly hiding underneath a lawyer's desk at an address I had scribbled on a note pad that was lying next to the phone.

How could this be possible? I went back inside and tried to shake off the strange phone call. Who was that on the other end of the phone if it had not been the neighbor lady? Why was she hiding in a lawyer's office after being arrested for a DUI? Wouldn't she have had to call me from jail? What was the one hundred dollars for? Why only cash? Why would she have asked me to dress nice? Why was she standing in her backyard at this very moment? So many unanswered questions surrounded me.

The phone rang again. I was hesitant to answer. It was one of my girlfriends. I told her of the odd call I received. She helped me work through it out loud. By the end of our conversation, I had brushed it off as just some really strange occurrence. I moved on with my day.

I received a strange phone call a month later. This one was much different. A man with a sexy broadcasting-type voice was on the other end this time. He made small talk and then introduced himself as a talent agent. He was looking for petite models to be the next-it girl. He knew I was the recipient of a few catalogs that featured beautiful young women dressed in the latest trending style in fashion. He knew I made purchases from those catalogs.

He asked me questions and threw in flattering comments. He made me blush and talk to him like a giddy school girl talking to her first crush. One phone call turned into two, which turned into three. I started to look forward to meeting the sexy-voiced stranger on the other end of the phone.

By the end of the week-long grooming conversations, he knew more about me than a stranger should. The reason I so willingly went along and just gave up this information about myself was because he was good at grooming a potential money-maker.

These were the days before cell phones and social media, so grooming was done by phone. I could have easily lied to him, but I didn't. For some strange reason, there was intrigue and excitement in speaking with him. He was promising me a future beyond anything I ever dreamed of. He made me promises of making money far beyond what I ever fathomed. I felt like I was soon going to be living the life of a fairy tale princess that almost every girl dreams of.

But things started to change. The man on the other end of the phone was becoming impatient with me. I did not agree to meet up with him after our first week of conversations. He started to slip. I soon began questioning this relationship. When I began asking him questions, he did not like it one bit. He became agitated. Now, when the phone rang, I wasn't hoping it would be him on the other end. I soon began to dread hearing his voice. What could I do? He would not stop calling.

During this time, I reached out to a news reporter who was well known for his exposés on scam artists. He suggested I record our conversations. After a few recorded conversations, he wanted to arrange a meeting where the reporter would then reveal his real motives. The reporter brought a recording device to me so I could record all of our phone calls. He gave me a list of questions I should ask. He suggested that I coax some answers from the mystery caller instead of him coaxing answers from me. I was ready to go full Nancy Drew. I was ready to turn the tables in my favor.

The next few phone calls, I was able to record our calls. I tried my hardest to extract information, but I was no match for him. It wasn't long before the man started calling shortly after I had arrived home from being out with friends. I was beginning to think he was watching my every move. I became paranoid that I was being watched like a wolf stalking his prey.

I soon realized I was in over my head. This is when I placed a call to a police detective for some real help. I knew this mystery man was up to no good. I wanted to stop him. I did not want to have him gloss over me and move on to the next girl. I knew there would be a next girl.

The female detective I was connected with was very nice. She agreed to work with me. She told me it would be difficult as he had not broken any laws. She wanted to keep it that way.

She told me to keep recording the conversation. She directed me to tell the caller that I needed to leave and get a number to call him back unexpectedly. I tried this tactic a couple of times, but to no prevail.

The detective then suggested we set up a meeting. She would meet with him instead of me. She would tell him he was treading dangerous waters and that he would now be the one stalked by police. She told me the meeting needed to be in a public restaurant. One that was heavily populated with a crowd of witnesses at any given point in time. I was nervous to take the conversations with him to this new level. The detective assured me everything would work out fine.

In the next few phone calls, we finally agreed to meet. Now, I was the one to lure him into my trap. I suggested that we meet a nearby Perkins during the daytime hours. He was fervidly against that location. He suggested a local park instead. I told him that a park was a strange place to meet a modeling agent of his degree. He confidently told me this happened all the time. He would bring his photographer to take some test photos. He told me to wear a short skirt and a low-cut shirt that exposed cleavage. He told me to look my sexiest, and I most definitely needed to come alone.

I pleaded with him to meet me at the restaurant. He told me the deal was off if I did not meet him where he wanted. He was calling the shots, and I should be agreeable to meet where he decided. He was about to change my life in the most unimaginable of ways. Frustrated, I agreed. He said he would call me back with a time and exact location.

After we hung up, I immediately phoned the detective and told her Perkins was a no-go. We needed to meet at a park. She said this was a horrible idea. She would not agree to it. I begged her, but she firmly said no. The only place this was to go down was at a public restaurant. If I couldn't make that happen, our little sting operation was over. We hung up. I wanted to cry. I'd come so close to exposing this person. I'd come so close to catching a bad guy.

I phoned one of my girlfriends and asked if she could hurry and come over to my house. I asked her if she was willing to hide in the back seat of my car in case I needed to be rescued from danger. In those days, video recording cameras were not small, discrete, or inexpensive. She would have to hide out and bear witness. I came this far; I was bound and determined to bring this man down, even if it meant I had to do it alone. I suddenly had the confidence of all three of Charlie's Angels.

She disagreed. She feverishly advised against it and told me to just let it go. I didn't want to do that. I was angry that she didn't have my back on this one. I felt abandoned by one of my best friends. I decided to follow through with this poorly executed plan on my own. I was sure that I could do this alone. I quickly got dressed in an outfit that was cute and sexy but not too revealing.

The entire time, I went back and forth on chickening out and abandoning this half-assed plan. I pretended like I was invincible. I felt I could take on the world no matter what. I did not realize how naïve I was being. I was about to embark on some real serious danger, and I thought I was Wonder Woman.

The phone rang. It was my mystery man. As we talked, he sensed my hesitation. It wasn't long before his tone changed. My hesitation grew larger by the minute. My womanly intuition finally set in. I was completely out of my league. Meeting this person alone would put me in a very dangerous predicament. One I wouldn't be able to charm or sweet talk my way out of.

The conversation spiraled me into backing out of the meeting with him. His anger boiled over. He revealed his true self at that moment. He began to berate me. He talked to me like I was an out-of-control spoiled child. The conversation ended with me telling him that I never wanted him to contact me again. I told him if he did, I was going to call the police. When I said the word police, he immediately hung up the phone. I felt chills run down my spine.

What just happened? I couldn't process it. I sat down on my bed and broke down into tears. How could I have been so foolish and naïve? I blamed myself and told no one. I put the entire ordeal in the locked and sealed memory vault of my mind.

I only saw Anna a few more times after this. She would just give me a big wave of the arm from the patio of her backyard. She never came over to visit again, and we never spoke. At the time, I didn't understand the reason for her suddenly blowing me off. I didn't give it a moment's thought that she was remotely involved in any of this. I never spoke to her about it. When the school year for the kids started, she flew back to England. The two of us never had contact again.

Today, online and social media platforms are the easiest and quickest way for traffickers to find victims. Traffickers infiltrate apps whose audience base is children. They use them to lure and groom their victims. Some social media apps have user term agreements that make it easy for child predators to navigate with ease and find prey. When a trafficker feels the heat from authorities, they can easily dump current profiles or platforms. They then switch to new ones without detection. They leave a continual cold trail and continue to conduct business as usual.

Besides social media, victimization is prevalent at casinos, hotels, highway truck stops, bus depots, and places where many people are coming and going. Places where someone's coming and going can easily go unnoticed and undetected. Places with a large crowd where victims can disappear into the crowd.

Some traffic rings, much like the one Jeffery Epstein and Ghislaine Maxwell ran, a trusted friend or acquaintance recruited victims. These recruiters are then rewarded with larger monetary payouts. As they get older and age out, the cycle from being trafficked to becoming a trafficker begins.

The bad news for traffickers is their victims are beginning to speak out. They are telling their stories of abuse and survival. They are warning others of the classic lines used to pull them in and the dangers of secret meetings with strangers. Their stories of heroic survival are becoming known with the help of advocates, podcasters, and social media. Undercover investigators, with the use of technology, are posing as bait to lure and capture these heinous criminals.

Classic evident signs of someone being trafficked are as follows:

- Appears to be controlled by someone
- Seems fearful and timid and avoids eye contact
- Is fearful of police contact
- Moves from city to city frequently
- Has signs of abuse: looks malnourished, high anxiety, has bruising or scars
- Has tattoos or brands that signify ownership
- Does not appear to have their own possessions

** If you know someone or suspect someone who is being trafficked, please call the National Human Trafficking Hotline at 1-888-373-7888

Audra

Say Her Name

(Her name has been changed for her protection)

"You can recognize survivors of abuse by their courage. When silence is so very inviting, they step forward and share their truth so others know they aren't alone."
— *Jeanne McElvaney*

Audra is an outgoing woman who loves the outdoors, sunsets, the smell of freshly baked cookies, and, most of all, her freedom. She is a woman who is in control of her life. Recently, she ran for public office because of her confidence and brutally honest opinions. She's not afraid to speak what's on her mind. But it wasn't always like that for her, not even close.

Audra was just a small child, not yet school-aged when she was stolen from her mother on an Indian Reservation. Her kidnapping was orchestrated by her biological non-Native father and his devious, vindictive, controlling, and top-notch crime-connected girlfriend. This woman assumed the role of Audra's mother. She was the only mother Audra would ever know.

Audra isn't sure who her biological mother is or if she's even alive. She has scattered memories of Pow Wows, hand games, and being on the reservation. She cannot remember their faces. Those have been erased by the years of abuse she's endured. Her biological father remained in her life but from a distance.

He was not allowed to get close to her. Even though he was a descendant of a famous mobster, his girlfriend had complete control over him. She called the shots. She extorted money from him. In return, he got to know the whereabouts of his daughter. He used his criminal connections to keep tabs on her. His girlfriend was also highly connected to criminals in all circles of life, from biker gangs' federal agents, and high-end politicians. Her connections were more powerful than his mafia connections from the days of old.

All the begging and pleading she did to get her daughter back were hopeless. He cheated on her and left her for another woman. A woman who was jealous of what they shared and took everything away from her.

With the odds stacked against her Native American Indian mother, the possibilities of seeing her daughter ever again were bleak. Falling in love with Audra's father was the biggest mistake she made in life. He gave her promises of a good life. Promises that were shattered. In the end, she lost the most precious thing she held near and dear to her heart.

The woman Audra was forced to call mom kept her continually drugged with phenobarbital. This enabled her to control and manipulate her into doing and going exactly where she wanted. By outward appearances, they looked like they were naturally mother and daughter. The woman had two older children that she also drugged in order to keep submissive as well.

What kind of mother would constantly drug her own children? A mother who is selling her young children into a child pedophile sex trafficking ring. Audra and her siblings were drugged by their mother and then prostituted out for cash, drugs, and sex.

Audra's mother was able to hide her crimes through her law enforcement and political connections. People who vowed to protect children against such heinous crimes were involved in committing the appalling crimes. They protected the people running the sex crime rings.

As a child, there was no way out for Audra and her siblings. She had no control of her life. She woke up every morning angry that she hadn't died in her sleep.

By the time she was ten years old, she was a drug addict. She was becoming tolerant to the drugs, and their effects were weakening. Her mother then gave her stronger, more addictive drugs to keep her submissive. The drugs were paid for and provided by the men who were paying her mother to have sex with her. A drugged victim will not fight back. A drugged victim is the easiest to control. Some of the men paid Audra's mother with sexual favors. They paid for sex with a child by having sex with her mother. Sometimes, they made payments in the form of drugs.

When Audra's two older siblings were old enough to make decisions on their own, they made the switch from abused to abuser. They began to help their mother provide partners for Audra and control her every move.

Audra was never able to have any real friends. She never brought a friend over to play at her house. She was never allowed to host a slumber party. The only people she was ever allowed to call friends, were people who provided drugs and raped her. They convinced her this was normal behavior. They told her this is what being friends was all about. Friends love each other. Friends never tell anyone what goes on behind closed doors. Snitches get stitches. Those words were made very clear to Audra her entire life.

Audra was moved from school to school. She can't even remember all the schools she's attended. There were so many. Her kidnapper only had her enrolled for about six or eight months at a time. Long enough to learn something but not long enough to make any real friends. It was always hard being the new kid at school, holding so many secrets. She was afraid to make friends. Any time she got close to someone at school, she was dis-enrolled. Her kidnapper would move her across town or send her to live with her relatives who were abusers involved in the same ring.

When she was finally old enough to be considered a dropout, she did just that. She wasn't allowed to go to school anymore. She was denied a proper education.

She was forced into marriage at sixteen. Her first marriage was to a twenty-five-year-old federal law enforcement officer. He and his sister had been providing drugs to Audra for many years. She had known him since she was a child. She knew him before he took an oath to protect and serve. Her first memory of him was when she was six or seven years old. He was just a teenager.

The woman she knew as her mother kidnapped a thirteen-year-old girl. Audra remembers sitting between her mother and her ex-husband, looking at the blue-eyed, freckled blond in the back seat. The girl was scared. Audra saw the teenage boy sitting next to her in the front seat of the car grab this girl out of the back seat by the hair. The girl was kicking and screaming. She was begging to be let go.

Audra witnessed him murder this teenage girl in cold blood. She remembers the girl's face. She remembers the horror of her screams and the terror in her eyes. He got back in the car, pointed the gun at Audra's head and said, "Not a fuckin word to anyone about this, or I'll have no problem killing you too."

The girl's remains were found a year later. Her murder remains unsolved to this very day. The threat to Audra remains the same. "Not a fuckin word to anyone about this, or I'll have no problem putting a bullet in your head too."

There is no witness protection for Audra. Her abusers are vastly connected. Her location would be pinpointed in a day or two. The headline in the newspaper would read, "Woman commits suicide at the ranch."

Audra's marriage wasn't the picture-perfect white wedding dress, June's bride marriage by any stretch of the means. Her marriage was one of control and continued abuse. She knew if she went up against him or turned him in, he'd have her thrown in jail for 25 years to life on planted drug evidence. He had access to enough drugs to get a solid conviction if he needed to.

She was trapped yet again. When she became pregnant with their first child, he weened her off drugs for the sake of their child. Being pregnant was her only salvation, so she had two more babies after the first one. What didn't happen, as she thought, was having children did not release her from her prison. It only made things worse as now she had brought children into a world she wouldn't have wished upon anyone.

When her children eventually became the right age, her husband had them dealing drugs and introduced them to the family crime ring. Audra escaped this living hell five separate times with her children to women's shelters. Each time, her husband showed up to retrieve her and told everyone it was nothing more than just a big misunderstanding.

The only way out of her dangerous marriage was the day when he took her hostage in their home. He held her hostage at rifle point until a pastor was able to negotiate her release. After a tense stand-off, he agreed to release her. She was finally able to file for and be granted a divorce.

She took the kids and headed south to start a new life. This wasn't an easy task as she had hoped. Her brother and sister still had their hooks on her and her children. They continued to have control over her. They watched her every move. Just when she thought she was away from one horrible abuser, she was thrust into a life with one who was worse than the last one. She was unable to break free.

Audra soon found herself in another marriage gone wrong. She had met a man who had romanced her and the kids. He promised her a life she had never known, and once she said I do, those promises came crashing down. She married a man she did not recognize. He wasn't the same man who had romanced her and convinced her to walk down the aisle with promise of a better life. He was just another narcissistic, criminally connected man. He was abusive towards her and her children. They went to live with their dad, who only had interests in turning his own children into drug mules and introducing them to a lifestyle they could never escape.

Audra's oldest son tried to escape the life of crime, corruption, and being controlled by his father. He tried to reach out and turn him in. He was about to tell everything he knew about his father and his crime ring and gave out names and dates. He was hiding out in a hotel room where he was supposed to be safe and secure.

He was found by his younger brother with a bullet in his head and a gun by his side. The death was ruled as a suicide; a convenient suicide. A strong message was sent to Audra and her other children about what would happen if they spoke out. Snitches get stitches or worse yet, "not a fuckin word to anyone about this, or I'll have no problem putting a bullet in your head too."

Audra's youngest son is currently in prison. About four months before her oldest son's death, her youngest son stole his dad's car, all the drugs in the house, and all the cash that had been stashed away. He thought taking everything and making a run for it would be his way out, but he was arrested, charged, and put in jail for crimes he never thought he'd ever be facing.

Audra's biological father passed away, and for reasons unknown to her, he made her executor to his estate. When she cleaned out his house, she found clues to her identity and her father's past.

She found photos of herself as a small child being held by an Indian woman with a date on the back of the photo that would have put her at around two years old. There were no names on the photos, just a date, but as she examined the photo, she recognized the child to be herself. She found other photos of gangsters from the days of old and several documents that helped her put together a map of her life and exactly who her ancestors were.

She could not find her birth certificate or documentation on who her birth mother was. She found a document that stated the woman who raised her had only given birth to two children, yet Audra was her third child. She wondered why her dad would have such a document. She had never seen her actual birth certificate. She didn't even know if one exists or where it is recorded.

Audra was driving home one night when, out of nowhere, a vehicle hit her head on. Two weeks earlier, Audra's older sister found out that she had control of her father's estate. She was putting the pieces of the puzzle of her life together.

Audra was rushed to the hospital. She does not know what happened to the driver who hit her. She doesn't even know who hit her. She's unaware if they survived the crash, perished, or walked away.

She was severely injured. She had a broken neck, a broken foot, a broken knee, and one of her hands was almost amputated. Screws and bars were placed in her neck and spine. C-4 through C-7 were fused.

She was bedbound for five months before she was able to rehab and move on with her life. She was supposed to die that night. Instead, she emerged that evening as a survivor. That night, she sent a message to her former abusers that she was invincible. She remembered the words of the woman who raised her. She was told her entire life, "Don't worry, child, you won't ever die".

Audra has since divorced her second husband and has moved on with her life. Audra is careful about who she gets close to and what information she shares. She's experienced so much loss in her life of those who got too close and tried to expose any kind of truth. Eight relative's deaths were ruled as suicide. Five friends of hers have died of mysterious circumstances. She's lost a son to a questionable suicide and a son to the prison system.

Even though she finally escaped by surviving an accident that was meant to take her life, she still feels like a prisoner to the lifetime of trauma she's experienced. She's not sure she'll ever truly be free to live a life where she's not being watched.

She knows her abusers have connections everywhere. Her motto to keep her going every day is "stay active and involved because if you fade into the shadows out of sight, it'll be easier to disappear suddenly."

Bad Boys, Bad Boys

Hell is empty, and all the devils are here.

~ William Shakespeare

⁖⁖

Police corruption has recently had a spotlight shone on it. To think it is something new is naive. Police corruption has been happening since at least the days of Al Capone in the early 1900s. Corruption isn't just something that affects major cities; it has also made its way to small-town America. Just like in the days of Al Capone, people who dare to internally challenge that corruption are threatened, set up, or chased out. While the vast majority of those serving to uphold law, order, and justice are good, decent, and upstanding people, there is the lion's share of corrupt individuals hiding behind the blindfolds of Lady Justice, giving the rest of the professionals a bad reputation.

Around the same time that Al Capone was wreaking havoc on Chicago, an up-and-coming town in California was having police corruption problems of a serious nature. Clint Eastwood showcased this in his 2008 film "Changeling," starring Angelina Jolie. Young boys were mysteriously disappearing in the town of Wineville. Southern California was booming at this time with the agriculture and film industry.

Christine Collins's son Walter was one of the boys who disappeared. He was just nine years old. A few weeks later, police reunited a young boy with Christine Collins. The only major issue was this boy was not her son. When Christine told police the boy was not her child, they told her she was still traumatized and under stress and that she was mistaken in recognizing her only child.

Christine challenged this, and the police chief deemed her a threat and a nuisance. She refused to back down on her claim. She had proof the boy they reunited her with was not her son. The police chief had her secretly thrown into an insane asylum and vilified her as being delusional and an unfit mother.

Eventually, she was freed, but only after the remains of several young boys were found on the property of a local chicken farmer. The town of Wineville had such a black eye from police corruption that the town's name was changed to Mira Loma to regain the public's trust in the town after corrupt officials were removed.

Fast forward to more recent times, a twenty-year history of crime was discovered in the Butte, Montana Police Department that ran from the late 1960s into the 1980s. Three officers were the ring leaders of criminal activity while they were on duty. They continued their run of corruption long after they turned in their badges.

They ran one of the biggest marijuana rings in the state of Montana. Not only were these three officers the drug kingpins of the state, but they were also involved in many other crimes without the worry of getting caught or being inflicted with potential consequences. They burglarized local businesses to the extent that the businesses were forced to close. They extorted two madams in order for the department to look the other way for their crimes of prostitution. One of the officers was even implicated in committing arson and attempted murder.

In Big Horn County, a former sheriff led the charge in 2008 to recall the current sitting sheriff, Lawrence Big Hair. Big Hair was facing allegations of incompetency, breaching the code of ethics, using prisoners to do private work and domestic assault. The upheaval of his elected position was unsuccessful, but the charges tainted his reputation. Even though the sheriff was Native American Indian, many feel he hadn't done much to help make things better.

Just a few months after Selena Not Afraid's disappearance, her father was named Big Horn County Undersheriff. He is a man of controversy in Big Horn County and on the Reservation. Not only is he related to the Sheriff, but there were allegations of molestation and abuse, which led to a restraining order from seeing his teenage daughter. He vehemently denied these accusations and was never charged with this crime, but this has tainted his reputation. He was removed as Chief Judge from the Crow Tribal Court in a 12 to 3 vote due to the Crow Judicial Ethics Board finding evidence of mismanaging tribal finances in 2018. It was found he was using tribal court funds as loans for his staff members.

Big Horn County's former coroner also owns the only funeral parlor in the county seat. He was brought up on ethics charges in 2003 when he embalmed a body without the family's permission. He then refused to release the body to the family until they provided payment for his embalming services. He used his role as the county coroner position to turn a profit in his funeral parlor. He was put on probation, fined, and required to take only eight hours of ethics classes.

The Big Horn County coroner cremated a young woman's body without permission from the family in the case of an 18-year-old local Native American Indian teen who went missing and was found deceased a few days later in 2019. According to the family, he stated this was the only way possible to release her remains to the family. He then told the family that he would be handling the funeral. He accepted payment from the family even though they wanted a different funeral parlor in a nearby town to handle the funeral arrangements.

The family was denied their right to a second opinion because she was cremated. They have never received a definitive cause of death. According to some locals these are not the only encounters of using his elected position for financial gain in his private business.

It doesn't just end there. In places like the Crow Reservation, the Northern Cheyenne Reservation, and the Big Horn County seat, rumors, allegations, eye witness accounts, video evidence, and the like are abundant. From the county coroner, local judges, county sheriff, tribal police, tribal council members, and tribal chairman, allegations of cover-ups, misconduct, and theft of federal money, drug schemes, and more have been circulating. In some cases, it turns out to be hearsay, but many times, sadly, the corruption has been proven.

Tribal judges have presided over their own child custody hearings after hours, and they have given lenient sentences to family members facing drug charges. In the circles of small-town America, it is no secret who is engaged in corrupt practices and who is not. Unfortunately, when it comes to elected officials in rural areas, the competition is sparse, and choices are few and far between.

Corruption and blurring the lines of the law don't just end with the police. They extend into the upper echelons of the law. A Montana State Federal Prosecutor, who was named Prosecutor of the Year in 2004, had his fall from grace in 2017. The U.S. Department of Justice and Office of Professional Responsibility began investing in him in 2014.

He was accused of misconduct, including hiding deals he made with key witnesses in exchange for their cooperation and testimony. He also granted immunity to key government witnesses in exchange for taking the stand while allowing the witness to say in front of a judge and jury that no promises were made in exchange for testifying. He was found guilty of wrongdoing in 2017 and was fired from the position but did not lose his license to practice law. He is currently a municipal judge in the county seat of Big Horn County.

An Intercept investigation into how federal prosecutors around the country are disciplined when they break the rules shows a secretive and flawed system. Despite public outcries and Justice Department promises to uphold accountability, there has been little reform. To this day, many federal prosecutors throughout the U.S. are able to escape misconduct charges, even after judges discover and determine that serious offenses were committed. Nicknames such as "roach motel" and "Bermuda Triangle" are used to describe the black holes where complaints against federal prosecutors are filed. The investigation showed that most state agencies are not tracking disciplinary action against attorneys properly.

An article written by a Native American journalist in Billings, Montana, outlined the culture of fraud in tribal politics. She articulated how tribal politicians are failing their people time after time. The article expresses that these downfalls are the primary reason why many rural Indian reservation communities remain stagnated with problems. The article's author uses her expertise to help people in these communities by introducing new forward thinking as a new movement striving to bring awareness.

White Buffalo - Bii'Shea'Chii'

If you want to be a sheepdog, you must make a conscious and moral decision every day to dedicate, equip and prepare yourself to thrive in that toxic, corrosive moment when the wolf comes knocking at the door.

~ Lt. Col. Dave Grossman

The first time I heard the analogies of sheepdogs, wolves, and sheep was at a Memorial Day service where Lt. Col. Mark Weber spoke of it in 2013. The next time I heard it was in the movie "American Sniper" just a year later. The analogy used was the same one written in the book "On Combat: The Psychology and Physiology of Deadly Conflict in War and in Peace," published by Lt. Col. Dave Grossman in 2004.

The analogy goes as such as told by Lt. Col. Dave Grossman: Most of the people in our society are sheep. They are kind, gentle, productive creatures who can only hurt each other by accident, and the vast majority of Americans are not inclined to hurt one another. The sheep have no capacity for violence and are healthy, productive citizens.

Then there are wolves. The wolves feed on the sheep without mercy. There are evil people in this world who are capable of evil deeds. The moment you forget that or pretend it is not so, you become a sheep. There is no safety in denial. The wolves have a capacity for violence and no empathy for fellow citizens. They are sometimes aggressive sociopaths.

Finally, there are sheepdogs. The sheepdog lives to protect the flock and confront the wolf. The sheepdog has a capacity for violence only if provoked but has a deep love for their fellow citizens. The sheepdog is a warrior. The sheepdog is someone who can walk into the heart of darkness, into the universal human phobia, and walk out unscathed.

The sheep generally do not like the sheepdog. He looks a lot like the wolf. He has fangs and the capacity for violence. The difference though is that the sheepdog must not, cannot, and never will harm the sheep. Any sheepdog who intentionally harms the lowliest little lamb will be punished and removed. The world cannot work any other way, at least not in a representative democracy or republic such as ours.

Still, the sheepdog disturbs the sheep. He is a constant reminder that wolves are in the land. The sheepdog's presence sometimes annoys the sheep. They would prefer he cash in his fangs, assimilate to their liking, and say "Baa." That is, until the wolf shows up. Then, the entire flock tries desperately to hide behind one lonely sheepdog.

There is nothing morally superior about the sheepdog; it is what you choose it to be. Also, the sheepdog is a funny critter: He is always sniffing around the perimeter, checking the breeze, barking at things that go bump in the night, and an older, wiser sheepdog is prepared for righteous battle at any given moment.

The sheep pretend that the wolf will never come, but the Sheepdog lives and prepares for that day. The sheepdog makes a conscious and moral decision every day to dedicate, equip, and prepare himself to survive the toxic, corrosive moment when the wolf comes knocking at the door. – *Lt. Col. Dave Grossman*

When I became acquainted with Cary Lance, it was evident that he is Big Horn County's sheepdog. Cary grew up on the reservation in Big Horn County. He's not of Native American

Indian descent, but his grandmother's half-brother was. His father was born and raised on the reservation.

Being one of the only white kids in town, Cary received his share of getting picked on and teased. When he was seven years old, one of Crow's elders decided to give the young Cary a new lease on life in order to survive on the reservation. He held a naming ceremony for him and gave him the name Bii'Shea'Chii', meaning White Buffalo. This name has stuck with him throughout his life, and the people in his circle refer to him as White Buffalo.

Cary's father taught him to weld in high school, and he would take this skill and join the Army as a metallurgist. After his time in the Army and working various jobs around the country, he returned to his hometown to re-plant his roots.

He began his role as citizen watch patrol known as Arrow Creek Community Watch in July of 2015 when the murders and attempted assignation of a couple and their teenage daughter rocked the community. He refers to that day as "my community's 9/11".

A couple was murdered in cold blood by an illegal immigrant who was on the reservation to buy meth from a local tribal member. This angered Cary. He made the decision to take action. No longer could he sit in his living room chair from the comfort of his home while people in his community needed serious help.

The lack of a visible police force has left an open door for meth dealers and other criminal activities. That tragic day was when Cary and five other tribal members, ranging from ex-soldiers to teachers whom he knew and trusted, picked up their weapons and assisted law enforcement in searching the district for the cold-blooded killer.

That evening, the group of five set up alternating watch shifts. Their mission was to slow the meth traffickers and criminals perusing the reservation. Getting his newly banded watch group up and running was met with its challenges.

Certain people did not like Cary patrolling while armed. Others, however, fully supported his right to carry for protection. He carries for self-protection and he only uses his firearms in self-defense. The reservation honors his constitutional right to carry and bear arms. He's had to go up against some people in the past who didn't seem to care too much if they were hurting innocent people or not.

Cary and his group are called upon to assist with a range of situations, including accidents, medical emergencies, livestock on the highway, people stranded in the nearby mountains, floods, storms, fires, and missing person searches. They also respond to reports of suspicious persons or activities.

His group operates with the help of donations. He and his crew patrol mostly on their own time and money. He is appreciated and loved by those he helps and protects. He is hated by the criminals he calls out by name. He strives to see that they are held accountable to the full extent of the law.

He told me the story about his first recovery. It haunts him to this day. Big Horn County emergency crews and the BIA searched for three hours for a five-year-old boy who fell into Pryor Creek. Cary suspects the young boy was pushed into the creek. He swallowed and choked on a piece of gum he was chewing upon hitting the water. The water was a chilly 40 degrees.

When Cary arrived on the scene, no one had actually gone into the water to search for the boy. They only checked for him from the dry banks of the river. Crews on the scene asked what they could do to help. He ended up locating the child twenty minutes after arrival.

He looked around and noticed that one of the trucks at the scene had a tiny boat loaded in the bed of it. Cary told the men to put the boat in the water and follow him. He jumped into the water and headed downstream. He found the boy downstream about 75 yards from where he had fallen in.

Floating face down, the child was stuck in some thick brush that was hanging over the water. It created a tunnel much like a surfer wave. As the boat pulled up behind Cary, he pulled the boy from under the brush and lifted him into the boat. An EMT on the scene tried using a CPR mask on him. Immediately, Cary had to instruct the EMT that he needed to roll him over, evacuate the water from his lungs and then start CPR. Basic training the EMT should have known.

Once the boy was secured in the boat, Cary pushed the boat upstream to where it was launched. By this time Cary's legs had cramped up on him from being in the ice cold much too long.

The EMT was able to get a heartbeat, and then the gum was found stuck in his throat. He was on the helicopter headed for a hospital when his heart stopped. The child's body was just not strong enough to endure all the trauma he had been through.

Little Steven was the youngest person Cary has had to recover and his hope is that he never sees someone that young again need his assistance.

The Arrow Creek Watch Group has grown as Cary has earned the trust of the broader community. He has established trusted relationships with local law enforcement agencies. His watchers are everywhere. They send him messages about any criminal activity. Many of the people relaying information on criminal activity wish to remain anonymous. Through time, local law enforcement has learned that the tips he relays to them are valid. They end up resulting in the apprehension of suspects. In February 2020, three violent criminals escaped from the Big Horn County jail. They were on the run for a few days. It was Intel from Cary's watch group that led to their re-capture.

Cary also helps monitor parolees. A large number of them end up back in prison as they have a hard time leaving meth alone. Meth is a huge problem on the reservation. He sees first-hand how it destroys people and families.

Cary is the reservation meth dealer's worst enemy. He is aware of who the dealers and users are. He knows what activities they are engaged in most of the time. He isn't afraid to call them out publicly, no matter who they are or how connected they are in the community. His goal is to get them banned from the reservation to stop his beloved community's suffering.

He has called out some pretty big names and has had the proof to back up his allegations. Doing this has put him in danger and his life at risk in the past. He showed me photographs when someone sent him an extreme message one night. They wanted to silence him by murdering one of his loyal, trusted, and faithful dogs. They also attempted to behead another one of his other dogs that same night.

The criminals crept onto his property in the cloak of darkness and attempted to saw the head of his dog off on his property. The local vet was able to save Cary's dog. He was left with a large vet bill and the reality that he was dealing with genuinely unmerciful people who were willing to stop at nothing to keep Cary from getting in the way of their criminal activity. This hasn't stopped Cary. He is determined more than ever to do his part to rid his community of drug dealers, thieves, and murderers.

Cary and his community watch group have recovered over 30 stolen vehicles. They have helped law enforcement capture fugitives from the law and provided useful information leading to the arrest of criminals. They help maintain peace during large events. They have assisted in countless recoveries of missing men and women.

One year after Hub Williamson went missing on the Crow reservation, Cary recovered his vehicle. The blue sweatshirt Hub was wearing the day he disappeared was lying folded in the car's front seat. The car was left in a field with the tires missing. The inside of the car was stripped out. Cary called the vehicle to authorities, who recovered the vehicle and are continuing their investigation into his disappearance.

Even though Cary receives hate messages and death threats on a regular basis, he will never stop caring for and protecting his community. The only compensation he asks for is knowing that the community is safe and that his group can give the families of the missing closure.

The Missing

The Search, the Wait, the Hope

Hub Williamson, Ashley Loring Heavy Runner, Jermaine Charlow, Aubrey Dameron, Diane Medicine Horse Rondeau, Freda Knowshisgun, Shacaiah Blue Harding, and Serenity Dennard; these are just a hand full of names of the missing where their loved ones have no answers and very little clues to their where-a-bouts. Amber alerts were not issued. Police investigations were poorly conducted or abandoned after no real clues or leads turned cold. The families are left solving the puzzle on their own.

The families are consumed by the desperate search for answers and the yearning to bring their loved ones home, regardless of the outcome. All they desire is closure. Until a body is found or the person walks through the front door, they live the nightmare every day and endure sleepless nights. They diligently follow every lead and pursue every clue, many of which turn out to be agonizingly false, further perpetuating the pain and suffering of those searching. As of January 27, 2023, the Montana Missing Person Database website currently lists 170 missing persons.

In March 2020, I heard about a fundraiser for a man who had gone missing in St Paul, Minnesota, from a friend in Montana. She shared a poster with details of an Indian taco fundraiser to raise money for search efforts.

He disappeared without a trace the month before. He walked out of his family home and vanished in the night. A month later, his daughter was hosting a feed in his honor to raise money for the continued search. His missing poster was just like all the others. A photo or two with a complete description containing age, height, weight, eye color, skin color, hair color, and other pertinent information. It also included phone numbers to call with information or tips.

As I walked up to the house, the smell of fry bread and taco fixings hit me like a brick through glass. People were in the front yard eating and conversing. The conversation was light-hearted, with strangers getting to know strangers. Everyone was there to help out a fellow human being who was working so hard to bring her father home.

I didn't know anyone when I walked up the sidewalk to her house. I had no idea about the reception I'd receive, being a stranger among the crowd. As it turned out, I wasn't alone.

Her post reached people she knew and also across state lines to people who didn't know her. We all came together with one common goal: to bring this man home so his daughter can finally have peace.

The hope and agony showed on her face. She stood at a table taking orders while her family made fry bread taco meat, cut up fresh vegetables, and whipped large batches of fresh guacamole.

I walked up to the table and placed an order. After I'd been there for a bit, I asked her if I could talk to her for a brief moment away from everyone. As we stepped aside away from the crowd, I could tell she was a bit nervous. Taking orders for the taco feed was a perfect distraction for her.

The money raised was to help continue funding the search. "We have no real leads, and I'm finding out money talks," she said as she rubbed her fingers together like she was shuffling dollar bills. The cold reality that people will extort a grief-stricken person for bits of information hit. She was going to do anything and everything she could to find her father.

We kept our conversation brief. She wanted this day to talk about the good things. She wanted to celebrate him. I think she knew at that point that he wasn't going to walk through her front door and say, "Hey everyone, I'm home!" She had succumbed to the notion that he was gone. She just wanted tangible answers. It was the not knowing that was tearing her up on the inside. It was the not knowing that took her mind to all sorts of places of her worst imagination.

She was doing everything possible to hold it together and not completely fall apart. It wasn't just that she had the job of working full time and raising a family, but she was burdened with the heavy task of searching for her father. She was the one helping everyone else hold it together, while inside, she was crumbling away each and every day.

Everyone helped stoke the small bonfire and withstood the feeling of frozen toes just to show support. The crisp spring air was keeping anyone from over staying their welcome. The fundraiser was dwindling down, so I ordered six Indian tacos to go. I threw in some extra money to help them fund the search. I walked to my car, with my arms full of food, hoping this man's search would soon end and the family would have their resolve.

I found out a few days later that on the evening of the fundraiser, she was notified by police that they had found her father. Now, the money she raised for the search would go towards funeral costs. She was so relieved she finally had resolve. The relief of knowing he was found was overwhelming. It meant that she would no longer have to worry daily about his where-a-bouts or if he was suffering. She was now filled with grief over his loss of life.

This St. Paul family was one of the fortunate ones to receive closure. Albeit their wait was long and grueling. There are still thousands of families trying to find anything, no matter how miniscule, to have closure to their endless days and nights that are filled with pain and emotional torment, Not knowing and not having the answers they long for.

They keep searching open fields, ponds, abandoned shacks, and back roads, hoping to find clues or evidence to end the nightmare. They continue to post missing flyers around town and on social media. They keep their loved one's name circulating so that they don't fall by the wayside and get buried and forgotten amongst the array of missing person cases. They stay vigilant as there is no other choice. They remain hopeful that one day, maybe not today, the next day, or even next week, but their search will be over one day.

** If you have any information on someone who is missing or whose murder has been unsolved, don't hesitate to get in touch with the Missing and Murdered Unit Tip Line. 1-833-560-2065**

Winds of Change

The Missing Children's Act of 1985, enacted in Montana, has done very little to help with the missing and murdered Native American Indians who have gone missing. Since then, laws such as Amber Alert, Brittany Alert, and the Silver Alert have been enacted, but still, many of the missing fall into the cracks of these systems.

It's almost impossible to imagine what it was like to get the word out when it comes to missing persons without the advances in social media and technology. During the late 70s and throughout the 80s a missing child campaign of a new kind was launched. Advocates and parents pushed for new ways to get the public's attention to help find missing children.

Anyone who lived in the 80s will probably remember seeing the faces of missing children on milk cartons. The dairy association wasn't the only group to display the names and faces of missing children on their products. Their names and faces also appeared on pizza boxes, grocery bags, and junk mail envelopes with the question, "Have you seen me?"

While the campaign was a great idea, in reality, it was not very effective in recovering missing persons. The milk carton campaign featured Caucasian children; most had been taken by a noncustodial divorced parent, not a stranger or acquaintance. The milk carton campaign brought an important awareness of "stranger danger."

Gradually, it was phased out and rendered obsolete. Not only did it instill fear in children, suggesting the possibility of their own abduction, but the lack of tracked data made it challenging to determine its effectiveness in locating missing children.

Amber Alerts replaced the milk carton campaign from the 70s and 80s.

An Amber Alert is issued when a child under the age of 18 has been abducted and is in danger of serious bodily harm or death. This alert requires law enforcement to confirm a legitimate abduction has occurred before it can be issued. An Amber Alert is not issued if law enforcement determines that the missing person left with their assailant willingly. This is extremely problematic in cases involving teenagers and adults.

A Brittany Alert, which is similar to an Amber Alert, is issued when an individual with a severe physical, mental, or developmental disability is reported as missing.

A Silver Alert is issued when an adult 50 years or older is reported as missing where the missing person has a clear indication of irreversible brain disorder, such as Alzheimer's or dementia.

What happens when a child, teen, or adult goes missing who doesn't fit the criteria of the above three mentioned alerts? The answer to that is shocking.

The answer is, "Maybe she's upset and spent the night at a friend's house?"

"Well, she ran away one or two other times and came back, so just wait a few days, and she'll come home again," or "She probably partied a little much last night and is waiting to come home until she sobers up."

Texas has a CLEAR (Coordinated Law Enforcement Adult Rescue) Alert program that was created through legislation in 2019. It is aimed at closing the current alert gaps. The criteria for meeting a CLEAR Alert is that the individual must be between the ages of 18 to 64.

A preliminary investigation should verify that the adult in question is in imminent danger of bodily injury or death. The CLEAR Alert request must be filed within 72 hours of the person's disappearance. Although Texas is the only state currently using the CLEAR Alert system, other states are looking to follow suit.

When the state of Montana focused time, effort, and resources investigating dead wolves rather than addressing the issue of missing and murdered Native American Indians, people decided enough was enough. Something needed to be done.

Due to recent injustices and the serious lack of meaningful law enforcement, activist, domestic violence, and sex trafficking survivor Annita Lucchesi decided to stand tall with the mothers of the community hardest hit by the missing and murdered epidemic.

The Sovereign Bodies Institutes, which Annita founded, has represented over 30 families in the region who had a loved one go missing or be murdered in Big Horn, Rosebud, and Yellowstone Counties of South East Montana. The Department of Justice in Montana shows this region of Montana has the highest number of MMIP cases, with Big Horn County having double the number per capita than the next highest county. Data collected by the Montana DOJ also shows that 71% of missing persons between 2017 and 2019 were under the age of 18.

The Institute gathers comprehensive data, raises awareness, and actively brings cases to justice. Too many times, the communities have seen the negligence of county sheriffs and coroners. Time after time, the families have felt ignored and unheard.

Savanna's Act, sponsored by Senator Lisa Murkowski, was passed in December of 2018. It was named after Savanna LaFontaine-Greywind from North Dakota. She was a member of the Spirit Lake Tribe. She was a 22-year-old visibly pregnant woman near her due date. She disappeared from her apartment near Fargo, ND.

Eight days after her disappearance, her body was found by kayakers. She was duct taped and wrapped in plastic in the Red River. Her unborn son was cut out and removed from her belly. He survived and was kidnapped.

Living in the apartment above Savanna, Brooke Crews meticulously executed the crime, driven by the deliberate intention to abduct Savanna's child through any means necessary. Her motive was to raise the baby as her own.

Savanna's Act directs the Department of Justice to review, revise, and develop law enforcement and justice protocols to address Missing and Murdered Native American Indians. The bill requires the DOJ to take the following actions: provide training to law enforcement agencies on how to record tribal enrollment for victims in federal databases. Develop and implement a strategy to notify citizens of the National Missing and Unidentified Persons System. Conduct specific outreach to Indian tribes regarding the ability to publicly enter information through the National Missing and Unidentified Persons System or other non-law enforcement-sensitive portals. Develop guidelines for response to cases of missing and murdered

Indians. Provide training and technical assistance to Indian tribes and law enforcement agencies for implementation of the developed guidelines. Finally, to report statistics on missing and murdering Native American Indians.

Alongside Savanna's Act, the Not Invisible Act also passed the senate in 2019. The purpose of this act is to increase intergovernmental coordination to identify and combat violent crime within Indian lands and among Native American Indians. A joint commission on violent crime occurring on reservations and against Native American Indians was to be established by the Secretary of the Interior in coordination with the Attorney General.

Savanna's Act and the Not Invisible Act are a huge step forward. More work for the missing and murdered Indian persons still needs addressing. A huge victory for the MMIP was Hanna's Act. Hanna's Act was sponsored by MT State Representative Rae Peppers of Lame Deer, MT, in April 2019. The bill was named after Hanna Harris, a vibrant 21-year-old single mother. She went missing on July 4th, 2013, on the Northern Cheyenne Reservation. Her body was found four days later, on July 8[th,] badly decomposed. Her remains were in such poor condition that her cause of death was never determined.

Hanna's family received answers to what had happened to their beloved daughter in March of 2014. The perpetrators of her death finally confessed to the crime of killing and disposing of her body. The couple who killed Hanna participated in the search party that Hanna's family organized while she was missing.

Hanna's mother and sister spent countless hours pushing for change. They testified in front of Montana Congress to get Hanna's Act passed.

Hanna's Act established a specialized missing person's position within the Montana Department of Justice, aiming to enhance coordination among diverse law enforcement agencies. The designated specialist manages entries into the database of the National Crime Information Center under the US Department of Justice. Additional databases are also utilized to ensure that records of missing persons are not only accurate but also comprehensive, emphasizing the importance of timely reporting.

Even with Savanna and Hanna's Acts, missing children still fall through the cracks. Children like Serenity Dennard, a 9-year-old South Dakota girl who lived in a residential youth home and had a history of running away. Under the cover of night, Serenity meticulously planned her escape by discreetly packing a suitcase. Strategically enlisting the help of a couple of friends to create a distraction, she seized the opportune moment to make her getaway.

Staff was unable to chase after Serenity, who had escaped the property, because they were attending to the children, causing the distraction. The staff called for help rather than chase her. Since she had run away and returned before, they didn't think the outcome would be any different this time.

Serenity came from a tumultuous background. Her birth parents were both sent to prison when she was a baby. She was bounced from one foster home to another foster home. She ended up living in a residential youth home in western South Dakota.

More than 66 agencies and over 1,200 people have logged approximately 5,246 miles searching for Serenity. Aircraft and K9 units were also used to assist with the search. Sadly, Serenity has been missing since that day in February 2019.

A petition started in 2019 to pass a law to enact the Serenity Alert is being passed around. It is short of the 500,000 signatures required to move it further. The Serenity Alert will be for children between the ages of newborn to 17 who were not abducted but are considered missing or endangered. It seeks to close the gap of the children who do not fit the criteria of having an Amber Alert issued. It would not include frequent runaways that would be considered not to be in any danger. It would cover children who were indeed abducted but do not fit the Amber Alert abduction criteria. It would not take the place of an Amber Alert. It will function on its own.

The Big Horn County Attorney Jay Harris launched a new task force just a few weeks after 18-year-old Kaysera Stops Pretty Places went missing on August 24, 2019. She was found in plain sight two days later.

In response to a concerning surge in missing and murdered Native American women, Montana families exerted pressure on local officials, prompting the creation of a dedicated task force to address the issue. Established with the assistance of The Looping in Native Communities Act, passed by the Montana legislature in 2019, this task force includes representatives from every Montana tribe as well as the Department of Justice. Originally set to expire in June 2021, this groundbreaking initiative received renewed support during the legislative session of the same year.

Two missing and murdered Indigenous People's executive orders were recently signed. The first order was signed in November of 2019. It created a national MMIW task force and response plan. The second order, named Operation Lady Justice, was signed in January 2020. Operation Lady Justice aims to erode the trend of missing and murdered Native American

Indians by implanting a multi-disciplinary and multi-jurisdictional team. It is to include consultations of tribal law enforcement with tribal governments to review cold case files.

This has many rejoicings. Some skeptics fear some will get lost in the cracks and that the goals are too vague. Advocates have doubts. The task force, composed of officials, leaves out indigenous survivors and families from the community. They also fear the leaders appointed to the task force will be the same leaders who have failed to serve justice in the communities. The faith and trust in elected officials are already strained.

February 3rd has been designated as National Missing Person's Day. May 5th, which is also Hanna Harris' birthday, has been designated as the National Day for Missing and Murdered Native Women and Girls.

These two dates give the nation an opportunity to bring awareness and change by expanding efforts with survivors, forensic experts, and law enforcement. Although these two days out of the year have been designated to this issue, it is a daily cause that needs recognition and resolutions.

Great strides have been made to address the missing and murdered indigenous people, but much more work is yet to be done. Social media is now the best tool for helping families bring home their loved ones. Five missing girls were found safe on May 13th, 2020. That was an unprecedented number for a single day. It was due to the diligence of families sharing their names and faces on social media.

Missing and Murdered Facebook sites are quick to post information on someone who goes missing. Updates are given when someone is found.

I Am Woman, Hear Me Roar

The lotus comes from the murkiest water, but grows into the purest thing.

~Nita Ambani

∴

Women have been working and forging the path to be equal to men for the last few decades. The women and the women's movement has been a powerful tool. Women have fought for the right to vote, the right to work, earn a decent wage, the right to choose their own careers, the right to compete in sports at college and professional levels, and so much more.

Women were not designed to be exact equals to men because we are not genetically engineered in the same way. Women were created to be and do what a man can't do. I think a woman's biggest superpower is to bring a life into this world, care for that creation, and mold and shape her child into a better version of herself.

Women are undeniably remarkable individuals. Reflecting on those who have played pivotal roles in shaping my life, I find inspiration in the incredible women who have been both mentors and friends, leaving an indelible mark on my journey. Considering the women in my bloodline with whom I share DNA, I am struck by their extraordinary ability to courageously overcome the challenges of their respective times. These women stood as pillars of strength, providing unwavering support and resilience for their children.

As I look at the matriarch hierarchy of the Indigenous Tribes, I'm reminded that women are the true force in making the world go around. We have strength and endurance beyond what we think we are capable of. Yet women are victimized and brutalized just because we are women. In some cases, it is women who do the most harm. The ones we trust the most are supposed to help and look after us.

Women are naturally caring, trusting, and nurturing creatures. Women can also be cruel, calculating, judging, vindictive, and cunning. Sometimes, women are crueler to other women than a man could ever be.

Women should build each other up and fix each other's crowns. We shouldn't compete against one another or tear each other down.

Women are jealous creatures. I believe it's in our nature. It's part of our protective side. I think that's why women are often compared to animals in the wild. We are called "mama bear" and "lioness." Watching either of these magnificent creatures in their habitat makes it easy to figure out why women are compared to them.

We all have a woman in our lives who has always been there for us through thick and thin. Someone who has lifted us up from our darkest hours. Someone who has provided support and let us shine in our best moments.

We all have an auntie, sister, cousin, or best friend who we can call at 2:00 am to rescue us from any situation we've gotten ourselves into. Perhaps she's been right next to your side in those great or chaotic times. We all have that friend who will hold our hair back when we're throwing up from natural or self-inflicted sickness. We have that one friend to whom we can confide our deepest, darkest secrets. We know that they will never be revealed to anyone and taken to each other's grave.

For every good woman in our lives, we also have a woman or two in our lives who has done nothing but cause trouble and drama for us. Yet we continue to have a relationship with these types of women, not understanding why we can't break that toxic tie.

There is the kind of girl who will leave you behind at the bar or party for their own selfish reasons. There is the kind of girl who will steal your boyfriend from underneath you. There is the kind of girl who you think you can trust to hold your deepest, darkest secrets, only to find that she'll turn on you. She'll tell every dirty secret and confession into the gossip for friends and strangers. She's the kind of girl who will have no reckoning of taking you down a spiraling dark path of self-destruction.

There is a certain code amongst female friends that, when broken, leads to chaos, drama, and infliction. Only the best of friends, the friendships that last decades, are the type of relationships in which you consider yourself more sisters than friends. Every woman deals with friendships on all sorts of different levels. These relationships help mold us. They make us the woman we are.

Some of us come out from bad relationships as stronger, more resilient women, having built walls not meant to be broken. Some come out on the other side of bad relationships as broken and shattered, with a path of insurmountable healing to achieve.

As I think about the Missing and Murdered Indigenous Women and Girls and hear their stories, oftentimes, there are women involved in the tragedies. Women who should have had their backs. Women who should have stood up for them. Instead, the women were culpable or participants in their deaths and turned a blind eye to the violence. Some of the women have kept silent about the violence they helped perpetrate.

But as I also think about the Missing and Murdered Indigenous Women and People's movement, it is women who are at the forefront demanding answers and justice. It is the women who hold vigil and go on searches.

The women are testifying in front of Congress about the need for justice and reform. It is the women who push for new laws to be written. There are plenty of great men standing by their sides in support. There are a few good men who spend countless hours and devote their time to assisting and arranging searches, but the glue of the MMIP/MMIW movement is the women.

It may be time for women to reconsider the focus of competition from striving to be equal to men to instead striving for equality among female counterparts. It's crucial for women to unite and support each other, stepping up as advocates and protectors rather than turning against one another. By resisting feelings of jealousy and rage towards fellow sisters, we can foster a collective strength and empowerment that benefits all women.

Every girl in this town is somebody's daughter.
An angel, a devil, no matter what they call her.
If they try to hold you down under that water,
Just come up baptized, baby; let it make you stronger

Trisha Yearwood

Jenny Pipe

Gathers with Horses Woman

∴

Where do I even begin with Jenny Pipe? This woman is such an amazing, incredible human being. As an outsider looking into her world on the reservation, she is making a bigger difference than she will ever give herself credit for. Jenny initially started a Facebook group to bring change to her community. The early inception of the group was positive. It wasn't long before the requests to join the group exploded and became unmanageable for one or even two people. She was surprised by the reception. It was bigger and more intense than she ever thought possible.

Due to her own safety, time management, and peace of mind, she had to take a break from it. She was being contacted at all hours by numerous people who needed her help. The original groups she started are now defunct; however, she continues to be the face and voice for change on the Northern Cheyenne Reservation.

Since gaining traction on social media, her presence is more than just a platform to expose corruption. Jenny utilizes it to connect with people on and off the reservation. She talks about and shows the current issues through video and opens the dialog for solutions.

She has covered a wide array of topics. I've watched Jenny talk about beauty tips, her own personal struggles, giving instruction on de-quilling a porcupine, and the importance of teaching Native youth about traditional Indian ways.

She has used the platform to bring awareness to the missing and murdered. In 2021, she drew people together to hold a vigil for all victims. One local man made a gigantic memorial wheel where people could come to put the names of their missing or murdered loved ones. Prayer ribbons were also placed upon the wheel. It was placed in the center of town for all to see.

The symbolism of the wheel is traditional. The wheel is an ancient and sacred symbol used by many tribes for centuries. The wheel has four areas of importance. It represents the four directions, the four states of being, the four sacred medicines, the four seasons, the four elements, and lastly, the four stages of life. It personifies the circle of life, the circle of self-awareness, and the circle of knowledge.

She has spoken about the tragedy of parents losing their sons and daughters to drugs and alcohol and the criminal way of life that often follows. This is a topic that she has a personal connection with. She is open and honest with the fact that her oldest son had lost his way and turned to a life that included alcohol and drugs. A lifestyle that she does not have tolerance for. She has one rule for her household that she will not bend on. No alcohol in the house. She's been firm with this rule, but that wasn't enough to keep her son away from peer pressure and running with the wrong crowd.

Jenny's back story begins like many others on the reservation. Her start in life is humbling and she has faced a lot of uncertainty and challenges. Her father was a Skid Row alcoholic. Her parents met when they were going to college to be drug and alcohol counselors. Her mother was her father's saving Grace. Her parents were prominent members of AA. She attended her first AA meeting with her dad when she was just four days old.

At the tender age of two weeks, she received the name Gathers With Horses Woman in a traditional naming ceremony orchestrated by her father's mother. This distinctive name has endured throughout her life. Despite harboring a fear of horses, an interesting paradox unfolds when her husband faces difficulty coaxing the horses into their corral. In a peculiar yet magical twist, he positions her in the middle of the corral, and miraculously, the horses gather around her with calmness and cooperation. In every sense, she proves to be a genuine horse whisperer, forging an inexplicable connection with these majestic creatures.

At the age of five, Jenny's dad passed away from a hereditary heart condition. This event turned Jenny's life upside down. Her mom became nomadic, thinking that a new town or a new home would change everything. New beginnings, new chapters in life, and new dreams.

Jenny learned to drive when she was only nine years old. This is not odd or abnormal for any country kid. Kids in the country and the reservation often learn to drive as soon as they can reach the pedals. She doesn't consider herself extraordinary for this. It's just something that was necessary for survival on the reservation.

All the moving was challenging. With each move, she was considered an outsider. Each move made it harder to overcome her undiagnosed learning disability of dyslexia. She was a good student, always receiving student of the month awards. With each move, she had to make new friends. Half-Breed, Dummy, and Big Mouth were all names Jenny was accustomed to hearing from peers. Name-calling did not break Jenny. She is a strong, resilient, independent woman.

Jenny has always had big aspirations in life. She wanted to be Miss Montana, Miss USA, Miss Universe and a NASCAR driver at the same time. She certainly could be any of those things.

Severe dyslexia caused Jenny to drop out of high school two weeks into her freshman year of High School. She has never obtained her GED, yet she is incredibly intelligent. A move to California in her teens, she learned how to be street-smart. She lived in Inglewood and Compton, California, where she learned to stand her ground. The streets of California are where she learned to fight not only with fists but also with her mind.

Outspoken since she could talk, Jenny has found herself in some precarious predicaments. Some she's had to physically fight her way out of. Some she mentally fought her way out of. With all of the trials and tribulations Jenny has faced, she has not succumbed to drug or alcohol addiction. She has tried them. It wasn't for her. Drugs and alcohol have a very negative effect on her. Tunnel vision and blackouts are the main reasons she abstains.

Willpower is a difficult trait for people with addictive personalities. Jenny's willpower is stronger than cravings. She understands that she has too much to lose by giving into addiction. She's not willing to risk everything. Her family and her mission in life are too important. She has seen first-hand the destructive ways of addiction. Smoking cigarettes is Jenny's vice. It's her addiction of choice. She started smoking when she was just ten years old. She swears she's going to die from smoking, but it helps keep her sane.

"Welcome to Cheyenne Truth Official Jenny's Shit Show." Jenny Pipe says at the beginning of every Facebook Live stream she does. She goes live whenever there is something on her mind that needs to get out. It doesn't matter what time of the day it is.

Jenny will throw on some sweats, put her hair in a messy bun or a ponytail, take a few drags of a cigarette and begin to speak. Her innermost thoughts come spilling out. Her group now has over 1,500 followers. I am one of them, and I have followed her since near the beginning.

Her live feeds are provocative, informative, and mesmerizing. You can't help but be drawn to her. I've never met Jenny. I did not grow up with her. I did not know who she was until I started to follow her Facebook page. I felt an instant connection to her. I felt her soulful spirit as I intently watched and listened each time she went live. I'd like to say that I've become friends with Jenny. I would even go as far as saying that she is my spirit animal.

She, like so many Native American Indians, is a collector of people. People are naturally drawn to her. She's real. She's raw. She's genuine. She's not for everybody. Especially those whom she exposes for sexual predatory behavior and corruption. Her candor and ability to listen are what draw victims of sexual assault to reach out to her with their stories.

She has had no formal training as a therapist, yet you would never know this. She carries the heavy mental burden of sexual assault victims with no real outlet but her Facebook page. She protects the identities of those who tell her the horrors of abuse, rape, and sodomy. She is trusted with these dark secrets. Instead of turning to a bottle for the euphoric release of such information, she goes to her yard, lights a cigarette, takes a deep drag, and begins to speak. This is her release.

She started her Facebook page when she was blocked from the Northern Cheyenne's Facebook page for asking questions about certain Tribal leaders. She wondered what they were hiding by blocking her. She hated being instantly shut down for asking really serious questions. Frustrated and annoyed, she began her own Facebook page to have it be an honest, open place to talk about issues facing the Northern Cheyenne People.

It's no accident that Sitting Bull is her direct descended grandfather. The quest for truth and transparency is encoded in her DNA. This lineage explains the fire and fight she has burning from within her. She's willing to die on a hill for a cause she firmly believes in.

In late 2020, Jenny faced one of the worst fights she had seen so far. She was exposing someone who had been charged by the FBI in 2015 for sexually assaulting a minor. By all outward superficial appearances, he is loved by those in high power positions, wears a full Indian headdress with honor, and even marches for injustice. Is he an honorable man or a sexual predator?

Jenny wanted to get to the heart of the matter. She started asking questions, and that's when his victims privately contacted her. She started openly talking about it. This was when she was contacted by his family. His family members invited her to their house to tell her to shut her mouth.

Intimidation isn't something Jenny gives in to. She knew she was walking into a trap, but she showed up anyway. She was scared and knew there was a chance she was going to lose, but that didn't hinder her. The victims of this man were scared, and he took something from them that they would never get back. This is where her fearlessness came into play.

Jenny's refusal to keep quiet and back down was met with a brutal attack. She was ambushed. She was kicked in the head with steel-toed boots, hit with a metal pole, kicked in the crotch, and spit on by someone who was COVID-19-positive. A woman involved in the ambush nearly bit Jenny's thumb off. She was on the ground getting kicked by six children; all the while, the elder of the family was on his front step holding a shotgun, saying, "Bring that White Bitch in the yard."

Bruised and bleeding, Tribal Police arrived and arrested her. They took her to Indian Health Services, who released her to jail. The court in Lame Deer set a bond, and she sat in jail for three days. Her husband and friends went to pay her bail. When they showed up, the courts said they had no paperwork, so they would not release her.

Being in jail on the reservation is like being in jail in a foreign country. She kept telling the correction officer that she was sick. She could not eat. She was burning up with a fever and had chills. She asked for antibiotics and treatment but was refused.

Her days in jail were lonely and miserable. She was deathly ill and in agonizing pain. IHS was mad at her. Correction Officers were mad at her. The court was mad at her. The people who jumped her were mad at her.

After spending three horrendous days in jail, she was released. She had a temperature of 104.9. Her husband rushed her to the hospital in Billings, Montana, over an hour away from her home. They took her immediately to surgery. Her thumb was septic. The Billings physicians were horrified by her injuries that were ignored by reservation jailers.

Bruised ribs, cuts on her body, a black eye, and an artificial thumb are no deterrent. If anything, this assault has made her focus stronger on her mission of calling out corruption and demanding real change on the reservation that is referred to by some of the locals as the "Sodomy Capital of the World".

Jenny continues to work for the change that is needed. She believes there is corruption with Tribal Leaders on the reservations because there is corruption on the federal levels outside the reservations. It's like a domino effect. The lack of consequences and judicial nepotism make it difficult to change.

She refuses to listen to the notion that this is the way it's always been, so this is the way it will always be. She doesn't care what people think of her. Being true to herself is what matters most. She will never waiver. She is led by what she feels in her heart and gut. She firmly believes her reservation can be Northern Cheyenne strong and proud. She knows to get there will take blood, sweat, and tears, all of which she has shed.

She uses the social media platform to show people on the reservation what is happening in tribal meetings. She attends them and records. I watched a public meeting where the tribal council wanted her to stop recording. The council member told her that she could not be recorded since she was not an enrolled member. She instantly handed her phone over to the person sitting next to her and declared, "There, now you are being recorded by an enrolled member of this tribe". This is her cry for transparency from Tribal leaders.

Keeping her social media page up and going is her way of telling everyone that she's not going anywhere. She's going to keep fighting the good fight because she knows that good always triumphs over evil. She will never stop Counting Coups in the modern world.

Selena Shelley Faye Bell Not Afraid

Say Her Name

June 18, 2003 – January 20, 2020

"When your life is falling apart, or you're at your lowest, just ride."

~Selena Bell Not Afraid

Ask anyone who knew Selena about her character; you will only hear positivity. Her family and friends recollect that she was a very intelligent young lady. She is described as wise beyond her sixteen years. She not only possessed book smarts but also had a strong sense of common sense. In addition to her intellectual prowess, she was an exceptional athlete and had earned the opportunity to become the first female rider for the champion Indian relay horse riding team. Her beauty emanated from both inside and out. The way she greeted people with a simple hello had a profound impact on everyone around her.

She was the kind of girl who was caring and protective. She was the caretaker, the glue, and the big sister to everyone around her. She was the one people sought out in times of need. She was the kind of girl who would drop everything to care for a needy friend. She even rode her horse, Wart, for miles to care for her grandmother when needed.

She was well-respected by her peers and the adults around her. Selena was a remarkable human, and her core of close-knit high school friends is nothing short of amazing. She wasn't irresponsible. She was the last person anyone would think would go missing. Her disappearance shocked the entire community to its core.

Selena was no stranger to adversity and tragedy. When she was young, she and her twin sister were caught up in a fierce custody battle between their parents. The intense conflict became a tipping point, which played an integral part in her eleven-year-old twin's suicide. Selena was the one who found her sister's body. She had hanged herself.

Selena had an older brother whom Billings Police shot on their front lawn. She also had an older sister who a hit-and-run driver killed. Losing three siblings to such violent means would be enough to cripple any young girl, but Selena was resilient. While the deaths of her siblings stayed with her, she rose above the tragedy. She was calm and the strength for those around her. She was the light out of all the darkness that surrounded her.

It was New Year's Eve, and Selena had made plans with a friend to hang out for the night. Deena was more than a friend; she was like a big sister. Deena had been good friends with Selena's older sister, Tristen. After Tristen's death, the two girls became close, even though Deena was seven years older. Deena looked after Selena, and Selena asked her for big sisterly advice.

Selena was excited she was going to hang out with Deena. She was looking forward to a quiet evening. She was thrilled to be ringing in the New Year, watching movies, enjoying pizza, and laughing with her sister, friend and confidant.

"Hey, Mom, can I get a ride to Deena's?" Selena asked her mother.

"Sure thing. I have got the car for tonight, but won't tomorrow. Is Deena giving you a ride home in the morning, or do I need to pick you up after midnight?"

"Deena would give me a ride home in the morning," Selena replied.

Selena skipped off to her bedroom to get herself ready for the evening. She decided not to pack an overnight bag as she slipped into her favorite pair of skinny ripped jeans. They were comfortable enough to sleep in, and she was going to be up most of the night anyway. She brushed her hair and applied a small amount of mascara. She didn't wear much makeup as she was a naturally beautiful girl.

After getting ready, Selena and her mom got in the car. As they drove towards Deena's house, Selena received a text.

"Hey Sal, change of plans. Come to my boyfriend's house instead." The text read with the address she was to go to.

Selena texted back, "Boyfriend?"

"Yeah, boyfriend. He won't be here until way later, though, so no worries." Deena texted back.

"Yeah, OK. See you there soon."

"Change of plans, Mom. Drop me off at this address instead." She held up her phone so her mom could see the address.

"Whose house is that?" Her mother asked.

"I guess Deena has a boyfriend now, so it's his house."

"Boyfriend? I thought it was just going to be you two girls."

"So did I."

"You still wanna go. I can turn this car around. We can order pizza if you want and have a girl's night of our own."

"Nah, thanks mom. It'll be alright. She texted and said he wouldn't be there until later anyway."

They arrived at the house and parked in front. Selena got out of the car and blew a kiss to her mom.

"Good night, Mom. Love you. See you tomorrow." Selena said as she turned around and walked into the house.

That evening was going along fine for the two girls. They enjoyed watching TV, laughing together, and talking about their boyfriends. Everything was perfect until the bars closed. Deena's boyfriend showed up with a bunch of people. They were ready to party.

These were not the type of people that Selena would hang out with. Selena was surprised that Deena was dating this wild boy. He wasn't exactly the type of guy you'd be willing to bring to meet your parents.

Selena figured he was a revenge boyfriend to get back at Deena's prominent parents. Suddenly, Selena was out of place. She was the only minor at a house party. She had no interest in drinking with them. She figured she'd just go to bed and get a ride with Deena in the morning as planned.

As the evening drew on, the party got a little too loud. The noise woke up the next-door neighbors, who had been fast asleep.

The neighbor woman nudged her husband. "Do you hear that?"

"Yeah, it sounds like fighting." He replied. "Do you think I should go over there and tell them to quiet down?"

"No, don't do that. That house is bad news. There are always cops over there. Call the police."

He dialed 911.

"Hello, 911, what's your emergency."

"Not really an emergency but the house next door is having a party. I think it is getting out of control. Lots of loud music, and it sounds like someone is fighting."

"Do you know who is fighting?"

"No, I don't. I can hear both men's and women's voices yelling at each other, though."

The cops arrived at Deena's boyfriend's house and knocked on the door. They were greeted by a single person with the door slightly cracked open.

"We got a call that there was a disturbance here. Everything OK." The officer asked.

"Yeah, everything's fine. Sorry if we got a little loud. We'll quiet down."

The officer tried to peer into the house. The person at the door closed the gap of the door between them a little tighter so he couldn't see in.

"OK, well, keep the music down. We don't want to have to come here again tonight," The officer said. He turned away and walked back to his car.

The neighbors peered out their window as they watched the exchange. They stayed up looking out the window after the police left to make sure no one from the house next to them came over to start trouble. Things remained quiet for the rest of the evening. The couple went back to bed.

The next morning, Selena's Aunt Cheryl called her at 9:00 am.

"Hey, Sal. Everything good with you?" Cheryl asked her.

"Yeah, it's all good. I'll be getting a ride home a bit later."

"Did you have a good time?"

"Yeah, well, sort of." Her voice faded off.

"What happened, honey?" Cheryl inquired.

"Deena's boyfriend showed up with a bunch of his loser friends. Otherwise, it was good."

"Ok, well, what time do you think you'll be home?"

"I'm not sure. I have to wake up Deena. She's still sleeping."

"OK, just let me know when you are coming. "

"Will do. Love you, Auntie."

"Love you two sweetie. See you later today."

Selena hung up the phone. She quietly stepped around empty beer cans, passed out partygoers, and tried to wake up a still-intoxicated Deena.

"Deena, Deena," Selena whispered as she shook her gently to wake her up. "I need a ride home. You promised."

"Sal, girl, relax. I'm in no shape right now. Let me sober up; then I'll give you a ride."

Selena was so upset and annoyed. Deena had never screwed her over like this before. This was so out of character for Deena. If she was trying to upset her prestigious parents by dating this guy, she was certainly succeeding. Selena did not like this guy or any of his friends. They were grade-A losers.

Deena finally got out of bed and got dressed. She was still in no condition to give Selena a ride home. She had way too much to drink, and the only thing she wanted to do was sleep.

At noon, Selena's mom called to find out when her daughter had planned on coming home.

"Hey Selena, you plan on coming home anytime soon?"

"Yeah, I need a ride. Can you come and get me? Deena's boyfriend showed up with a bunch of people, and they all got drunk. They are still drunk."

"What?"

"Yeah, I know. I'm so mad at Deena right now."

"OK, I'll be there as soon as I can. I'll call you when I'm on my way. "

"OK, love you, Mom. Thanks."

At 12:15 that day, Selena's mom tried calling her to let her know she'd be on her way soon. Selena did not answer. Her mom tried calling her a few times. There was still no answer.

She drove over to Deena's boyfriend's house to pick up Selena. She was hoping that her daughter missed her call because she was in the bathroom or something simple like that.

When she arrived, Selena was not there. She saw Deena half passed out in the car in the front driveway. She shook her head as she walked past and into the house. What she saw astounded her. There was no way her daughter could be associated with any of this. The house was a mess; someone was throwing up in the bathroom. There were empty bottles of alcohol everywhere. It was a complete disaster. She returned outside, where she found Deena slumped over in the vehicle.

"Deena! Deena!" She shouted in Deena's face. "Where's Sal? Where's my Sal?"

Deena incoherently stated, "She got a ride with my boyfriend and some others. They are headed back to Hardin."

Selena's mom left very angry at the situation she had just seen. Everything she saw was completely out of place for Selena. Nothing made sense. She had a bad feeling something wasn't right. She decided she would go home and wait.

She paced the floor, anxiously awaiting confirmation that Selena had safely reached her grandmother's house in Hardin. Selena attended school in Hardin, residing there during the week, while on weekends and holidays, she stayed with her mom in Billings, just fifty miles away. Given that she had school the next day, tagging along with Deena's friends, who were heading towards Hardin, seemed like a sensible choice.

However, it puzzled Selena's Mom that she hadn't waited for her arrival. Selena was aware that her mom was on her way to pick her up. Why would she leave with other people? The situation wasn't making sense to Selena's Mom, and she found herself contemplating every possible scenario. A sense of unease lingered despite her attempts to convince herself that everything was fine.

Another hour and a half passed and there was still no word from Selena. The drive from Billings to Hardin is less than an hour's drive. Selena's mom called her sister Cheryl.

"Hey Cheryl, you heard from Sal."

"No, not recently. Just earlier this morning."

"Hmmm… Something's not right. I know it."

"What's going on? Is everything OK?"

"No, something's wrong. Something's very wrong. I can sense it. I just know it." Her voice started to shake.

"OK, hold on. Talk to me. What's going on?"

"It's Sal. She called me about noon and needed a ride."

"I thought she was getting a ride from Deena?"

"So did I. Turns out Deena's got herself some new boyfriend. Deena was half passed out in her car in the front yard when I arrived at his house. "

"What?"

"Yeah, can you believe that shit? That girl, what a letdown. I'm so angry with her. She was supposed to be hanging out with Sal, not throwing some big house party."

"There was a party?"

"Oh yeah, you should have seen the place. I'm going back there. Something's not right."

"No, don't go. Call the police. Let them handle this."

"Yeah, right, like they handle everything else?"

"Well, let me make some calls. I'll be right down there. Hold tight. I'm sure Sal's fine. We'll find her."

Selena's mom hung up the phone and got back in her car. She drove back to the house and stormed through the front door. She started demanding answers.

"Where's my daughter!?" she screamed at the few people who were half asleep on the couch. They just looked at her, not knowing what she was talking about. She walked from room to room, trying to find anyone who might know. Deena told her she'd left the house, but there was no sign of her.

Why hadn't Selena contacted her yet? She should have by now. Enough time had passed for her to have arrived safely in Hardin. As she searched around the house, she noticed there was a pillow in the bedroom that had some blood on it. She couldn't tell if it was fresh or dried, but it was a noticeable red stain. She panicked and started searching around even more. She entered the bedroom and found Selena's purse lying there. She picked it up and looked inside. It was indeed Selena's, just as she suspected. She tucked it under her arm and stomped into the living room.

"Get up, you assholes!" She yelled at a person who passed out on the couch. "Where the hell is my daughter?"

The young man on the couch slowly opened his eyes and looked at her. He rubbed his eyes and sat up. The smell of booze permeated his body.

"I don't know, man. Quit freaking out. Geez. Stop yelling at us. She left a while ago."

"With who? When?" She started blurting out questions.

"I don't know, man. There were like five or six of them. They all left and went to Hardin. They are probably there by now."

Not getting the answers she needed, she marched out the front door, flung it open, and stomped out. She picked up her phone and dialed Cheryl.

"Cheryl, something's definitely wrong. I found Selena's purse at this house. Everyone says she left about two hours ago. Have you heard from her? Why would she leave her purse here?"

"I'm calling the police, and I'll see you in a bit."

A broken-down green minivan pulled into the Hardin trailer court about two and a half hours after it departed from Billings. Out of the six people who had left Deena's house in the van, only four were present. Selena and another girl were missing.

According to the remaining occupants of the vehicle, the van broke down at a rest area approximately twenty miles outside of town. They informed the police that while they were waiting for assistance, Selena and the other girl became upset and ran off into the fields. The occupants claimed that after the girls left, the van mysteriously started up again, allowing them to drive to Hardin. When it was time to depart, Selena and the other girl were nowhere to be found, so they left without them. When news circulated that Selena and another girl had left the rest area, a flood of people made their way to the rest area to look for the girls. Time was of the utmost importance. Selena's mom, Selena's aunt, and police showed up to look for her.

Phone calls were made, and more people showed up to join the search. The Bureau of Land Management arrived with drones. A family from a nearby town arrived with a helicopter. Local people came to assist with the search on foot. The

Sheriff's Department had a truck at the rest sight with its sirens wailing. They were calling out to the girls with a bullhorn. Three hours after Selena spoke to her mom, a well-organized search for the teen had begun.

Word was received on this first day that the woman who ran into the field with Selena had been located. Another vehicle had arrived and picked her up, but Selena was not with her. She did not know where Selena was.

Cheryl, Selena's mom, and others stayed in the rest area. They hoped Selena would see or hear them and make her way back. They did not leave the rest area the entire night.

The next day, January 2, people arrived with side-by-side ATVs. BNSF Railroad arrived with drones that were equipped with high-tech thermal imaging. They had the capability to sense and detect heat from people, animals, and stressed vegetation. The drone's thermal imaging is able to detect a body suspected to be slightly decomposed or buried in a shallow grave. People arrived with horses to help cover more distance. People arrived with campers. They brought food and water to assist the searchers and help comfort a very worried mother and aunt.

January 3rd brought more searchers, including Cary Lance and his crew. Word got out that she had not been found, so many more people arrived to assist. The school bus driver brought a busload of her classmates to help search the site.

Selena was a presence they were missing. Classes were not the same without her. No one could focus in class, knowing that Selena was out there somewhere needing help. Family, classmates, friends, and strangers were searching relentlessly, following every clue.

As each day passed with no word on Selena's whereabouts, more and more people arrived at the rest area to assist in the search effort. People were camping out, keeping watch and searching continuously around the clock. Campfires were stoked all evening long. Coffee became a staple of life. Not a moment passed when someone wasn't searching. Police, BIA, and the FBI made their appearances, but they didn't put in the time or the effort equal to what the volunteers conducted.

Word started to spread about the five people that Selena was last seen with. Police questioned them and they gave conflicting accounts as to what had happened that day. Their stories changed the more they were questioned. Their names were circulating, and people were watching their every move.

Deena's boyfriend and another girl were seen by several people packing up their belongings and leaving town. Deena's boyfriend went to Florida. He stayed there for a few months until things settled down. Two others were involved in a crime elsewhere. They lied to police so often that investigators and county prosecutors had to throw the case out. They were unreliable witnesses.

Around town and at the rest area people were putting the pieces of the puzzle together. They were finding that things were not adding up. A couple of social media Snap Chats had been posted the day she went missing but were quickly deleted. They were later recovered by clever people who knew the girls who posted them.

One photo showed a woman holding a Corona beer bottle on what appeared to be blood-stained blue jeans. Another video showed Deena's boyfriend arguing with a woman. You could see a woman in the video with long black hair. Her face wasn't visible, but some say they heard her voice. Her arms appeared to be pushing Deena's boyfriend away as he knocked a ball cap off her head. You couldn't see her face, but some say they heard her voice. The video was slowed down and examined frame by frame. What was originally said to have taken place at the rest area did not match up with the background in the video.

After a week had passed, Selena's story was catching national attention. Word of her disappearance was spreading like wildfire. Pressure was mounting on the police, the BIA, and the FBI. Family, friends, and volunteers were losing their faith in a system that has failed them time and time again.

Cheryl was doing everything in her power to keep the search going. She had to remain steadfast as the pillar of strength for Selena's mom. She became the voice to keep Selena's story going. She would not give up until Selena was found one way or another.

Her story was swirling all over local and national news. It was the talk of every town in Montana. Her story was circulating on social media throughout the country. National networks such as CNN, The New York Times, and HBO were covering her story. Her face was almost everywhere.

By day eight, there was a sharp turn in the weather. The weather had transitioned from beautiful, sunny, and pleasant 40-50 degrees to temperatures below 30 with an unsympathetic typical Montana winter wind.

On the twelfth day of Selena's disappearance, the Missing Person's Task Force took over leading the search. They had all the equipment in order to continue. Cheryl and Selena's mom decided that there really wasn't much more that they could do. They were exhausted and needed a break. Twelve days of camping out at the rest area, sleeping in their car, and searching endlessly was taking a toll. The search effort seemed futile for twelve long, exhausting days and nights. Cheryl was going to leave it in the hands of the task force that arrived. They seemed to have their act together, and it seemed like they knew what they were doing.

As the next few days passed, the task force widened the search area. They came up with nothing, so they moved their search area to another grid. They abandoned the rest area search site after it was scoured for two weeks. People packed up and left. Selena was not there. The search area grid turned up with nothing. High-tech thermal imaging drones that had spotted rabbits, field mice, and other small land animals. People on horseback, helicopters flying overhead, ATVs and people on foot all found nothing.

The search area spread further from the rest area to other sections of the rural area. It seemed unfeasible for a teen to have wandered that far.

Cheryl and Selena's mother were updated daily on the progress. Each day, there was nothing but the feeling of defeat. They were beginning to wonder if Selena would ever be found and if they were ever going to get a resolution for her disappearance. Nothing about her disappearance made any sense.

Cheryl knew somebody had to know something. She was going to keep putting pressure on every law enforcement agency, and the people last seen with Selena. She was going to find the answers. Cheryl put pressure on one couple that had last seen her. She asked them to come forward and tell the truth. They started leaving her threatening messages and told her that she had to shut her mouth.

After eighteen days of futile searching, a twenty-man FBI search team arrived. They scanned and re-scanned areas already covered by volunteers. They extended the search area in hopes of finding something. Anything that may have been missed by volunteers or local officials.

January 20th, approximately one mile from the rest area, in the sage, wild prairie grass landscape laden with rocks and gopher holes, the Bureau of Land Management, with the assistance of search dogs, found Selena out in the open of that vast field. Her body was found 30 yards from an old farm road that is well-used and accessible from the rest area where the van broke down just twenty days earlier.

She was lying on her back, with one arm flat by her head and the other arm straight up in the air. Her left leg was bent at a peculiar angle. She was not wearing her jacket or shoes when she was found. Those items of clothing were not found near her body and have never been discovered. Two of the three rings that she always wore and never took off were found in two separate locations approximately 20 yards from her body. She had what appeared to be bruising with thick lines extending upwards on her neck. The searchers had to cross several barbed wire fences to get to her where she was lying.

Cheryl and Selena's family were notified by a local news station rather than by law enforcement that her remains were found. The Big Horn County Sheriff immediately ruled her cause of death as 'accidental hypothermia, no foul play' before an investigation was even conducted. A toxicology report determined that Selena's blood alcohol content was 0.0. She was 100% sober when she went missing.

News of the discovery of her body, the condition in which her body was found, the circumstances of her disappearance, and the rushed judgement as to her cause of death caused a huge uproar throughout the community. Selena was the 29th person to have been reported missing in Big Horn County. She was the fourth girl whose cause of death was determined as unknown or accidental hypothermia in less than a year.

Selena's tragic death has sparked a fire in the Missing and Murdered Indigenous People's movement. It's undeniably shocking and unfortunate that she was the 29th young indigenous person to have gone missing in Big Horn County. Her death became the tipping point to bring attention to a problem that is happening right under our noses in Indian country.

Her death has caused a ripple effect, bringing awareness, demands for justice, and a louder voice for the missing and murdered. However, young Native American Indian women are still going missing every day at an alarming rate.

Heartfelt words by Selena

1.) I love horses, I love everything about them their eyes, the way they breathe, the way they move. I mostly enjoy riding, feeling free in the wind as I feel four feet beneath me. I love race horses, Me and My grandmother are raiseing race horses If we aren't home we are most likely at the barns with our horses. My grandma always told me growing up "when your life is falling apart, or youre at your lowest, Just ride" — Selena Not Afraid

2.) I'm the youngest of five siblings. I love my family deeply. can't wait tell we all reunite!

3.) I have a twin sister(s) and older sister(s) who passed away in 2014 and 2018. Life's never been the same but I still have hope. My twin died of suicide. My sister died of a hit n run. I'm still trying to process this.

4.) I love to bead, and sew creature, My whole family does it. I feel like it's part of me. I love dreaming in my creativity.

5.) I also really like to bake with my mom, I'm slowly learning more and more from her.

6.) We lost my elder brother two years ago on Nov 18th 2017 infront of my house, he was shot 17 times by Billings PD. He was only 23 yrs old, I miss him dearly. Just glad he had two children.

7.) I love to travel to different horses races W/grandma.

8.) I no enjoy reading really anything.

9.) I have one sibling left, I plan on going to college close to where he lives.

10.) I really hope one day I will builto my own barn and have race horses, cows, A stud

Epilogue

Sadly, Selena Not Afraid was not the last young person to disappear under mysterious circumstances. She was not the last Native American Indian from Big Horn County to have gone missing or been murdered. Mildred Old Crow, Christy Rose Woodenthigh, and Ky-Mani Vega Little Bird are just a few of the names that have made local headlines since Selena was found.

Big Horn County Attorney Jay Harris has released the following public statement in 2021. "Big Horn County is undeniably a community in crisis. Tragic, unnecessary deaths, along with the many reports of missing persons, are major alarm signals to a community in crisis. It is past time our community's embrace of life and demands for justice amidst the many issues associated with Missing and Murdered Indigenous People be recognized as the modern civil rights cause for our generation."

As the years have long passed, I look back at the experiences I've lived to tell. I'm really amazed that I have survived many things. When I think back on the crazy things I did when I was young, I think of how lucky I am. Nothing severe has happened to me. I'm sure many of us can reflect and say the same.

How many times did I take a ride from strangers? How often did I go to a party where I barely knew anyone? How many times did I put myself in a precarious situation that could have left me beaten, dead, or never found?

It was the days before social media, cell phones, and technology. I could have easily fallen victim to numerous scenarios. When I think of the women featured in this book, I can easily find something in my life that is relatable to each and every one of them. I wonder if I were a young person now and did the same exact things I did in the 80s, would I be alive to tell the tale? I really don't think so. I certainly would not have survived if I was a Native American Indian woman living on the reservation.

How does life choose who survives and who doesn't? We will never know this answer. It is a question that will never be answered.

I often wonder if we were safer in the 70s and 80s than now. Are we simply more aware now due to social media that did not exist back then? Back then, there were no cell phones or social media. We didn't take selfies. We did not post every moment of our lives on Instagram and Snapchat. I don't recall hearing of women in my community rampantly going missing or turning up dead like they are now.

I ask myself why we are more disconnected from each other now. People are inherently good, but everyone has a dark side. It seems like that dark side is showing up more and more. When are we going to say enough is enough?

When are we going to no longer accept mistreating friends with disrespect and leaving them stranded to die? When are people going to take responsibility for their actions? When are we going to hold people accountable for their actions that leave young Native American Indians gone way before their time? When are we going to say something or do something if we see something we know is not right? Every day we wait, and every day we sit idly by, another Native American Indian woman, girl, man, boy, or child goes missing. One more flyer is created. One more family grieves. The time is here; the time is now. Say something. Do something.

Notes from lectures 11.13.2024

- 1st book on the Mayan? Also self published & edited, not proud of it but used those learning to do this one with a editor
- 5 awards for this book.
- Orginally tried tradtional publishing but numerous rejected ode to subject matter So she self published with a credit card, well reviewed and awarded
- Sold in 6 countries in only English
- Stories were reviewed by the subject / family spokesperson so nothing surprised them
- Identifies as white but a community member. Grew up with the town
- Selena's story was a catalist for the community to talk to her
- Wrote it during Covid doing all the interviews with facetime and phone
- Not working on another, Just forced on this one and getting in translating
- Drive for this book was to the community to get the story out
- Sheriff in the book no longer the sheriff (which is a good thing)
- Changes in law informe.
- If she wasn't already part of the community, she doesn't think the families would have written
- Available in audiobook, her niece did the reading and production in SD.